KAMALA
HARRIS

Leila Rasheed

Illustrated by **Sarah Papworth**

SCHOLASTIC

Published in the UK by Scholastic, 2021
Euston House, 24 Eversholt Street, London, NW1 1DB
Scholastic Ireland, 89E Lagan Road, Dublin Industrial Estate, Glasnevin,
Dublin, D11 HP5F

SCHOLASTIC and associated logos are trademarks and/or
registered trademarks of Scholastic Inc.

Text © Leila Rasheed, 2021
Illustrations by Sarah Papworth © Scholastic, 2021

ISBN 978 07023 1233 5

A CIP catalogue record for this book is available from the British Library.

Printed by CPI Group (UK) Ltd, Croydon, CR0 4YY
Paper made from wood grown in sustainable forests and
other controlled sources.

1 3 5 7 9 10 8 6 4 2

www.scholastic.co.uk

CONTENTS

INTRODUCTION:

A COUNTRY OF POSSIBILITIES

"WHILE I MAY BE THE FIRST WOMAN IN THIS OFFICE, I WON'T BE THE LAST — BECAUSE EVERY LITTLE GIRL WATCHING TONIGHT SEES THAT THIS IS A COUNTRY OF POSSIBILITIES."

Kamala Harris, *This is a Country of Possibilities* speech (2020)

A New Day

On 20 January 2021, as the Covid-19 pandemic raged across the world, Joseph "Joe" Biden became the forty-sixth president of the United States of America. Joe Biden was a seventy-eighty-year-old white man from Delaware on the East Coast of the USA. He had been a senator, representing his state of Delaware, for many, many years and he had been vice president of the USA for eight years under President Obama. He was a familiar face at this kind of event and had been to this ceremony at the Capitol building before. He was the kind of person that Americans were used to seeing become president. It felt like the country was going "back to normal" after a chaotic four years.

His second in command, however, was a complete contrast. Kamala (pronounced Karma-la) Harris – an energetic Black woman with a big, confident smile and a determined expression in her eyes – was much younger, only fifty-six. She had only been a senator for a few years, and she was from the opposite coast of the USA: the San Francisco Bay Area. Just a few moments before the new president took his oath, she had taken hers.

Kamala Harris was now the forty-ninth vice president of the USA. It was the most powerful position that any woman in the USA had ever been in. If Joe Biden represented "back to normal", Kamala Harris represented "things are different now".

The special ceremony where a president and vice president are sworn in is called an "inauguration". The word comes from ancient Rome, when a priest called an "augur" would carry out rituals to discover whether the gods were happy with the people's choice of leader. In the USA, Inauguration Day is when the person who won the presidential election months before, makes a promise to the American people that they will be a good leader. Only when they have made that promise – called the Presidential Oath of Office – do they really become the president. The vice president has to swear an oath of office too. They will be the second in command to the president, and take over from the president if they become unable to do the job.

Inauguration Day is an exciting and joyful time, and people come from all over the USA to be part of celebrations in the capital, Washington, DC. The new president and vice president make speeches, and there are prayers and performances by the best musicians, poets and speakers in the USA. There are also celebrations, balls, parades and parties leading up to the day itself. Traditionally, the previous president is there to show support for democracy and the role of president, even if they aren't happy about giving up the presidency. People get together and share a sense of hope for the future. Some things were the same as usual for Joe Biden and Kamala Harris on Inauguration Day 2021 – but many were not.

PROMISING TO PROTECT THE CONSTITUTION

There are performances, prayers and parties on Inauguration Day, but swearing the Oath of Office is the only part of the day that absolutely has to happen! The president puts their hand on a Bible and repeats these words:

"I do solemnly swear that I will faithfully execute the Office of President of the United States, and will to the best of my ability, preserve, protect and defend the Constitution of the United States."

The Constitution is a document that the people who first founded the United States of America in 1776 wrote, to say what their country should be like. The Constitution wasn't perfect – it famously spoke of liberty and equality, but left out anyone who wasn't a white man. Over time, it has been changed and improved. Every time a president is inaugurated, it continues a history of democracy in the USA that started with the first words of the Constitution: *"We, the People of the United States..."* meaning that the USA was going to be a country ruled not by kings and queens, but by its citizens.

U.S. flag

An Inauguration Day Like No Other

In early 2020, the Covid-19 virus had begun spreading across the world and soon reached the

USA. There was no cure and, at that point, no vaccine. Millions of people were falling ill and dying, as the virus passed easily from person to person. That meant that big gatherings of people were out of the question – even for Inauguration Day. Instead of the big, noisy parades through Washington, DC, and shows of support from celebrity singers, actors and performers, there were virtual concerts and events on social media. The number of guests and spectators was limited, too. Usually, the public would have been invited and the Mall, the grounds of the Capitol building, thrown open so the atmosphere was like a rock concert. But there was no way that could happen in 2021. Instead, the few invited guests – mostly politicians and family members – wore masks and had to stay two metres (six feet) from each other. The sight of some of the most powerful people in the world freezing on fold-up chairs and wearing face coverings, was far from the usual image of celebration. The knowledge that so many people had died in the last year made the mood much more sombre than it should have been. But Covid-19 was not the only shadow hanging over the day.

Dangerous Days for Democracy

The themes for Inauguration Day were "America United" and "Our Determined Democracy: Forging a More Perfect Union". They had been chosen carefully, because just a few weeks before, American democracy had seemed in awful danger. The United States was far from united. Although the Democratic Party had won the election, the former president, Republican Donald Trump, had refused to accept the results. He said, with no proof, that the election had been stolen from him.

On 6 January 2021, he made a speech to thousands of his supporters in front of the Capitol building in Washington, DC, where the elected lawmakers of the USA were counting the final votes. He basically told his supporters to fight against the result – and so they did. The crowd turned and marched down to the Capitol building. They stormed the building, smashing windows, breaking things and overwhelming the police. Shockingly, five people died before the army and police got control and stopped the violence. Many of the thousands of people who had attacked the Capitol were white supremacists – racist people who believe that white people are better than anyone else and should have power over those who are not white. The mob had carried racist flags and shouted racist slogans.

There were threats of violence on Inauguration Day, too. People were worried more riots might ruin the event. It was against this background that Kamala Harris, surrounded by security and in front of an audience who all knew there was a chance of another attack, stepped up to take her oath of office as vice president. Placing her hand upon a Bible, she swore to defend the Constitution and to do her job well. With that promise, she became:

- the first female vice president of the USA ever
- the highest-ranking woman in American politics ever
- the first Black American vice president ever
- the first Asian American vice president ever.

It was a strong and hopeful contrast with the violence of just a few days before.

UNITED STATES PRESIDENTIAL ELECTIONS

The USA is a democracy, which means that Americans get to choose their leaders. It is divided into fifty states that make their own laws. However, these states are all part of a "federation" or group (the United States of America). There is a national government in Washington, DC (the federal government). The president lives in the White House, but the Senate – very important politicians – meet and work in the Capitol building.

The president is a leader for all Americans, and represents the whole of the USA to the rest of the world. They are also the leader of the armed forces. As vice president, Kamala

Harris might have to take on these powers in an emergency, for example if President Biden were to die suddenly. There is a presidential election every four years, and presidents are not allowed to be elected to office more than twice (two four-year terms).

In an American presidential election, political parties choose who they want to be their candidate for president. The presidential candidate then chooses the person they want to be vice president. The two sets of candidates then run for election against each other.

The USA is a big country, with lots of small political parties such as the Reform Party and the Green Party but most people vote for one of the two big political parties:

DEMOCRATS

Democratic policies are generally progressive. Often Democrats want to change laws to reflect modern times. They think the government should be involved in people's lives. Democrats usually support free health care and want more controls on who can carry guns.

Founded in: 1828

Famous presidents: Andrew Jackson, John F Kennedy, Barack Obama

Symbol: a donkey – this started as an insult from their enemies, but the Democrats decided they liked how donkeys symbolized ordinary, hard-working people and took it on!

REPUBLICANS

Republican policies are generally conservative. Often Rebulicans want to hold on to the old ways of doing things. They think the government should not tell people what to do. Republicans usually support lower taxes, restrictions on who can immigrate to the USA and the right to carry guns.

Founded in: 1854

Famous presidents: Abraham Lincoln, Richard Nixon, Donald Trump

Symbol: an elephant

VPOTUS

20 January 2021 was an inauguration day like no other, in good ways and bad ways. Kamala Harris was a vice president like no other, too. Born in 1964, the same year that the Civil Rights Act was passed (see page 26), Kamala Harris' life had been shaped, as the years went on, by increasing opportunities for women and people of colour in the USA. Even before she became vice president, during her career as a lawyer and a politician she had achieved many things that were exceptional and often unique for any American woman, let alone a Black woman, who had to struggle against racism as well as sexism. She was clearly a talented, driven and special person. Even so, becoming vice president of the USA (often shortened to VPOTUS) was an extraordinary achievement that not everyone had expected from her.

On 20 January 2021, she proved any doubters wrong. It was an incredible journey for someone who was the child of immigrants and had not been born into a family who were part of the world of American politics. So where did she come from and how did she get here? Who is Kamala Harris?

ROOTS AND CHILDHOOD

A Family Who Fought for Civil Rights

Kamala Devi Harris was born in Oakland, California on 20 October 1964. Both her parents were immigrants, meaning they moved to the USA from other countries. Kamala's father, Donald Harris, was from Jamaica. Kamala and her sister were brought up mostly by their mother, Shyamala Gopalan, who was from India.

In India, a caste is a life-long social group, into which someone is born. Shyamala's family were in the highest caste, known as the Brahmin caste, and so enjoyed a lot of privilege. Shyamala's parents had always encouraged their children, including their daughters, to be independent and have a career. Shyamala herself graduated from the University of Delhi at a time when few girls in India went to university. Soon after, she applied to University of California, Berkeley, to study for a PhD. In 1960, this was a big step for her to take. It meant Shyamala would not get to see her family for years as travel was so expensive, and she had no relatives in the USA.

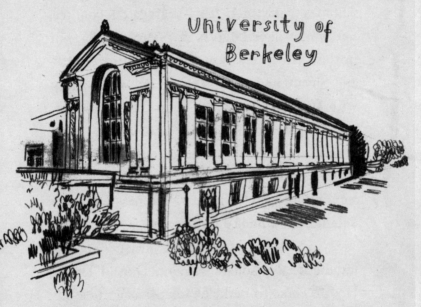

University of Berkeley

There was a lot to get used to for Shyamala. In the USA at this time, Black and white people were segregated – or kept apart – by many laws. Buses, bathrooms, hotels, restaurants and schools could all be segregated, with some for "whites only" and some for "Blacks only". It was the white people in government making these laws and usually the facilities and opportunities for Black people were much worse than those for white people.

As an Indian, Shyamala had to work out where she fit in in this segregated country. She might have been high caste in India, but in the USA it was skin colour that mattered – and Shyamala was not considered white. Even with the support of her family, following her chosen path in life would have taken steely determination, an adventurous spirit and readiness to fight for what she valued. They were qualities which she would pass on to her daughters, Kamala and Maya.

At Berkeley, Shyamala met another international graduate student, Donald Harris. He had come to Berkeley from Jamaica to study for a PhD in economics. Shyamala and Donald had many things in common: their intelligence, their experience as immigrants to the USA, their love of music. Above all, both were fiercely committed to fighting for justice and equality, so both became part of the civil rights movement.

It was how they first met – at protests, meetings and marches which were focused on making the USA a fairer and more equal place. They fell in love and got married.

Donald Harris and Shyamala Gopalan

WHAT ARE YOUR CIVIL RIGHTS?

Civil rights are the rights that every person has to be treated equally. They are your rights not to be treated worse than others because of things like your skin colour, religion, gender, sexual orientation or disability. They include the right to vote, to have an education, to be paid equally for equal work. They include the right to safety, to life and to freedom of thought and speech. They include the right to have any religion or none, and to move around your country and the world.

An Important Year

It was a big year for the USA in 1964, and for Shyamala and Donald too. It was the year Kamala was born. It was also the year that Shyamala was awarded her PhD and became a doctor of science. And it was the year that the Civil Rights Act was passed. This was a landmark law that made it illegal to discriminate against people because of their race, skin colour, religion, sex or national origin. All the marching and the protesting had ended in victory for people like Shyamala and Donald. Now they had a baby daughter, the future looked bright.

However, Kamala's parents were growing apart from each other. As a young child Kamala was saddened to see her parents becoming unhappy and angry with each other. They stayed together for a few years and even had another baby, Kamala's younger sister, Maya. However, they finally separated when Kamala was five years old.

Kamala's father, Donald, took a job teaching at the University of Wisconsin, and Shyamala began working in the cancer lab in Berkeley's Zoology department. She found a place to live with Kamala and Maya, in a city near Berkeley called Oakland. Oakland, named after the oaks that once grew in the region, is a bustling and lively city and port in California. It was the place that Kamala would come to think of as her home. It would also shape her as a person – Oakland was a special place in which to grow up.

WHAT IS THE CIVIL RIGHTS MOVEMENT?

The civil rights movement in the USA is the combined efforts of Black Americans and their allies to end racism and allow everyone to have equal rights to voting, health, education and more. The movement had its roots in the abolitionist movement, which fought to bring about an end to slavery. Long after slavery had been abolished, life in the USA continued to be unfair for many Black Americans. Systems designed to keep power in the hands of white people barred Black Americans from having the same rights and opportunities as their white neighbours. It was not until the 1960s that the Civil Rights Act proposed by President Kennedy, making discrimination illegal, was finally signed into law – thanks to activists like Kamala's parents. This meant that places and organizations, including schools, buses, restaurants and employers, were no longer allowed to turn people away based on the colour of their skin. However, even afterwards, there was a long struggle to get some states and individuals to respect the law, and this struggle continues into the present day.

A Home in Oakland

Shyamala knew that even though she was Indian, her children would be seen, in the USA, as Black Americans. She brought them up in a tightly knit Black community in North Oakland. North Oakland had a proud history of fighting for civil rights – it was the birthplace of the Black Panther Party, an activist group which was famous for taking direct, often violent, action against racism. The area Kamala grew up in was called the flatlands, contrasting with the wealthier areas in the beautiful hills of San Francisco.

Kamala had a happy childhood. She grew up

surrounded by her mother's friends, many of whom were university lecturers and activists who fought for equal rights. Her nursery school was run by a woman named Mrs Shelton who became like a second mother to Kamala and her sister. At nursery school, Kamala learned about great Black American leaders, speakers and thinkers such as Frederick Douglass, Sojourner Truth and Harriet Tubman. Mrs Shelton built Kamala's confidence until she believed she was capable of anything. Kamala remembered her nursery teacher all her life. Later on, as a politician, she would put early childhood education at the top of her list of things she thought were important and could change the world for the better.

Harriet Tubman

Changing the World by Bus

When they started school, although Kamala and Maya lived in Oakland, they were "bussed" to school in a different city as part of a desegregation programme. Segregation had been made illegal in 1964, but even years later many school children remained separated by skin colour because their families had been forced to live in different places depending on whether they were white or Black. Some children were therefore driven by bus to schools in a different area, so that white and Black children could get used to going to school together. Kamala was one of these children. She and Maya went to Thousand Oaks Elementary School, one of the first primary schools in Berkeley to be desegregated.

Kamala continued to visit her father on weekends and holidays. With him, she also visited their family in Jamaica. Donald encouraged her to explore the island, and the pair had a warm relationship. However, it was her mother who was her main carer throughout her childhood. Shyamala was supportive and loving but always expected the best from her daughters. She always told them they could achieve anything they wanted if they worked hard enough.

DONALD HARRIS
(1938–PRESENT)

Donald Harris, Kamala's father, is an economist – someone who studies the part of society that creates wealth through the buying and selling of goods and services. He was born in Jamaica, and although he is now a professor at Stanford University in the

USA, his identity remains proudly Jamaican. It was his grandmothers, Christiana Brown and Iris Finegan, who sparked his interest in economics through the practical work that they did in business and farming. Listening to their conversations about politics made him wonder how Jamaica and other developing countries could become wealthier and allow everyone to benefit from that wealth. For many years, he advised the Jamaican government and its prime ministers on how to run the economy. Throughout his career he challenged traditional ways of thinking about economics.

"IT IS UP TO EACH GENERATION TO PLAY ITS PART, USING WELL THE LEGACY IT INHERITS FROM THE PREVIOUS GENERATION,

> ## SO AS TO LEAVE BEHIND SOMETHING OF VALUE FOR THOSE WHO FOLLOW."
>
> Donald Harris, *"Reflections of a Jamaican Father"*,
> *Jamaican Global Online* (2018)

Indian Roots

"I AM WHO I AM. I'M GOOD WITH IT. YOU MIGHT NEED TO FIGURE IT OUT, BUT I'M FINE WITH IT."

Kamala Harris, interview with
The Washington Post (2019)

Kamala did not meet her Indian grandparents for a few years; air travel between the USA and India was still more difficult and expensive then than it is today. Her grandparents had not even been able to afford to fly to the USA for their daughter's wedding. They did not have a phone line in the house, so they communicated with Shyamala and their granddaughters using aerograms. These pale blue, pre-paid, printed sheets were a well-known sight to migrant families in the 1960s to 1980s. They could be folded up, sealed and posted off quickly, without the need for an envelope which would have made the letter heavier and more expensive.

In the late 1960s and early 1970s, Kamala was finally able to fly out to see her grandparents, and Shyamala was able to introduce her parents to her two daughters. Kamala visited her grandparents first in India and later in the new nation of Zambia, where her grandfather was posted as a diplomat on behalf of the Indian government.

PAINGANADU VENKATARAMAN GOPALAN (1911–1998)

Kamala's grandfather, Painganadu, was born in a village in Tamil Nadu, India into a Brahmin family. He had an arranged marriage, which was very happy, to Rajam, Kamala's grandmother. Rajam supported victims of domestic violence and helped Indian women learn how to look after their health. They had four children.

Painganadu worked in the Indian civil service – the office of adminstrators whose job it is to make politicians' ideas become reality. He rose to a high level, and later became a diplomat – someone who carries out work for the government, and helps to make and maintain friendly relationships with other countries. He was sent to work in Zambia, which was a newly independent nation. There, he organized the movement of refugees from Southern Rhodesia (now named Zimbabwe) into Zambia. After this role came to an end, he was appointed advisor to the president of Zambia. To Kamala, he was a beloved grandfather with a great sense of humour, who also inspired her with his honesty and hard work.

Once she met them, Kamala quickly grew to love her Indian family. As she grew older, her grandfather's honesty and disapproval of corrupt officials made an impression on her. She and her grandfather wrote to each other often over the years until his death in 1998. She later said her grandfather was "one of her favourite people in all the world".

Kamala grew up feeling comfortable with her Indian and Jamaican heritage. She knew others might find her mixed identity confusing or strange, but that was their problem, not hers. In her own eyes, she was simply an American. As Shyamala told her daughters:

"DON'T LET ANYBODY TELL YOU WHO YOU ARE. YOU TELL THEM WHO YOU ARE."

Kamala Harris, recalling Shyamala Gopalan's advice, *ABC News* interview (2019)

GROWING UP

Kamala the Activist

....

"WE HAVE A LOT OF WORK AHEAD OF US. LET'S GET STARTED."

Kamala Harris, Twitter™ post (2020)

Activism and protest were part of Kamala Harris' life right from the start. Her parents used to take her in a pushchair to civil rights marches. It was thrilling to be surrounded by the energy and enthusiasm of the marchers, a crowd of people who all wanted the same thing: change for the better, justice and freedom. Right from the start of her life, she understood that things in the USA were not fair, and that she could do something to change that.

Kamala's mother often took her daughters to a cultural centre called the Rainbow Sign, in Berkeley. It was a spectacular place, based in an old funeral parlour, with chandeliers, vaulted ceilings and an organ loft. There were performances, a cinema room, an art gallery, a dance studio and a café. With performances by people such as Nina Simone, there was always something going on to celebrate Black culture, thought and art and encourage pride and awareness of the achievements of Black men and women in the USA. There were concerts, poetry readings, performances, art and plenty of good food in the restaurant.

Nina Simone

The Rainbow Sign warmly welcomed children and Kamala loved it there. She loved the powerful speakers and singers and the audiences who answered back. Her mother was always telling her to fight systems to make them fairer, and that success meant helping others to achieve things too. At the Rainbow Sign, Kamala saw all kinds of people who were putting that advice into action.

Shirley Chisholm for the People

In 1971, when Kamala was seven years old, Shirley Chisholm visited the centre. She was the first Black woman to try to get a major party – the Democrats – to pick her to run for president of the USA. Her campaign slogan was "Unbought and unbossed". By this, she meant that she

BRING U.S. TOGETHER

VOTE CHISHOLM 1972
UNBOUGHT AND UNBOSSED

would not take bribes or be bullied into making bad decisions.

Shirley Chisholm was a strong, fierce and smart woman. However, she didn't get much support from inside her own party, the Democrats. From outside it, she got death threats from people who didn't think a Black woman should dare to dream of becoming president.

When she announced she was going to run for president, Shirley Chisholm told voters: "I am not the candidate of Black America, although I am Black and proud. I am not the candidate of the women's movement of this country, although I am a woman and equally proud of that. I am the candidate of the people." It was a position that Kamala Harris echoed years later in her own presidential campaign when she said: "You want to talk about women's issues? That's fantastic. Let's talk about health care, education, climate change, and more." A Black, female president could be everyone's president. Women's issues were everyone's issues. Civil rights were everyone's rights.

Although Shirley Chisholm did not win, she

broke new ground for people like Kamala Harris to build on. Chisholm was a "first" – someone who made it possible for the USA to even imagine a Black woman president. This was less than a decade after the Civil Rights Act and only four years after the Supreme Court had ruled interracial marriage legal. Kamala Harris, years later in 2020, would echo Shirley Chisholm's presidential campaign in her branding, as a mark of respect, acknowledging the woman who forced open the doors of opportunity she was walking through.

SHIRLEY CHISHOLM

Shirley Chisholm was born in Brooklyn, New York in 1924, to parents from Guyana and Barbados. Her father was a labourer and her mother was a seamstress. At that time there were still plenty of people alive who had been enslaved. Segregation was fiercely defended, especially in the southern states of the USA.

As a child she was sent to live in Barbados with her mother's family, where she learned to be confident in herself. When she came back to New York, she began working in early childhood education.

In the 1950s Shirley became involved in Democrat politics, and in 1964 she was elected to the New York State Assembly. Things were changing, and in 1968 she became the first Black woman elected to the United States Congress. In 1972, she tried to run for president. But it seemed that America wasn't ready for a change that big. She later said: "When I ran for the Congress, when I ran for president, I met more discrimination as a woman than for being Black." Her bid for president was unsuccessful. A short while later, her husband was seriously injured in a car accident and she decided to retire from politics to care for him. She returned to teaching and used her role to encourage students to accept others' differences. Although she never made it to president, in 2015 she was posthumously (after death) awarded the Presidential Medal of Freedom, one of the USA's highest honours.

Presidential Medal of Freedom

Not Just an Activist

"MY MESSAGE TO THE MANY WOMEN WHO WILL CONTINUE TO BREAK BARRIERS AND BE 'FIRSTS' IN THEIR FIELDS IS: DON'T GIVE UP, BELIEVE IN YOURSELF AND LET YOUR TALENT LEAD YOU."

Kamala Harris, *"Ilhan Omar, Kamala Harris, and More on the Privileges and Pressures of Being a Political 'First'"*, *Harper's Bazaar* (2020)

Kamala loved her home in sunny California. But then her mother was offered a job at McGill University in Montreal, Canada, and they had to move. Montreal could not have been more different to San Francisco Bay. The weather was cold and snowy. The language in school was French. Kamala never felt settled. However, when she packed her suitcase she hadn't forgotten her activist attitude! At her new school, children weren't allowed to play football on the field, so Kamala started a protest. The protest won a change in the rules. While they were living in Montreal, too, her mother gave shelter to a school friend of Kamala's who was being abused by her stepfather. It made a great impression on Kamala, and defending women and children against abusers would become one of the things that mattered most to her throughout her career.

It never occurred to her not to have a career. Everyone she admired, men or women, worked hard and loved their jobs. But what did she really want to do? She was sure she did not want to be a scientist like her mother – she was more interested in the arts and in politics. Above all, she was interested in making the world a better place.

Kamala knew she wanted to make a difference. She believed in equality and justice and in the civil rights movement. However, she knew from early on that being just an activist was not the right path for her. Activists could only try to influence the powerful. She wanted to be the person with the power – above all, the power to help. Kamala knew that she wanted to be someone that others could rely on; the person they called in an emergency. For her, the way to do that was to become a lawyer.

WHAT IS AN ACTIVIST?

An activist is a person who believes strongly in political or social change and works to make this happen through activities such as public protests, campaigns and direct action. Famous activists who have fought for a range of causes from women's rights to the environment include **Mahatma Gandhi** (civil rights), **Greta Thunberg** (the environment), **Malala Yousafzai** (women's rights), **Emmeline Pankhurst** (women's rights) and **Dr Martin Luther King Jr** (civil rights).

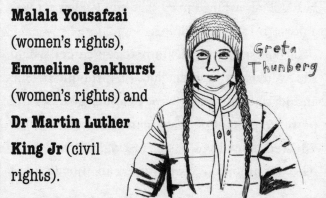

Greta Thunberg

Kamala the Lawyer

Why a lawyer? Well, when they needed help, Kamala's family and friends often turned to the lawyers they knew. Lawyers had brought about changes that made life better for millions of Americans. Kamala's greatest heroes were lawyers – one of them, Thurgood Marshall, had founded the NAACP (National Association for the Advancement of Colored People) Legal Defense Fund in 1940. This was a pot of money used to defend the rights of Black Americans who were accused of crimes, and who could not afford a lawyer to represent them. Without a good defence, in front of a jury who were racist, they were often unfairly judged guilty. The NAACP showed Kamala that being a lawyer was a powerful way of helping.

Of course, law was also an exciting career, where she would get to meet lots of different people and learn about their lives. It would give her the power to protect people and make decisions that affected many lives. It was just right for someone who was ambitious, determined and not afraid of a tough challenge or responsibility. For Kamala, justice was important, and having a real effect – making a difference – was important. She was never willing to wait if she could make something happen herself.

Kamala already knew where she wanted to practice law, and it wasn't in Montreal. She wanted to work in California, and especially in the Bay Area, where she felt her real home and community was. The first step was to head back to the USA and get a degree at a great university. So, after graduating from high school in 1981, she went to study at Howard University

Howard University

in Washington, DC. Howard was a "historically Black" university – one which had been created when Black students were not allowed to study at the same universities as white students. As a result, the fight for civil rights and for fair treatment for everyone was built into its bricks. It was also the same university that her hero, lawyer Thurgood Marshall, had studied at. Kamala could not wait to get started!

Being a Lawyer

While some people might imagine that being a lawyer is about studying and memorizing facts from books, it is about much more than that. As a lawyer you have to know what you are talking about, of course, but you also have to have the confidence to stand up and put your views forward in front of a judge and jury, and be good enough at debating to win an argument. Your performance in court could put someone in prison or keep them out of it. Kamala had to learn that sort of confidence – and the resilience to deal with losing. She had to get experience in putting her point across and persuading people to trust her.

While at Howard University she ran for office for the first time: asking her fellow students to vote for her as freshman (first year) class representative on the Liberal Arts Student Council. She also joined the debate team, a club where students hone their public speaking skills by taking part in competitive debates about various subjects. Kamala also joined a sorority, a club for female students, called Alpha Kappa Alpha. In the 1980s, law was still seen as a man's world. Women going into law would need to be able to hold their own against sexism, so good friendships made through a sorority were important for keeping your spirits up. She also took on plenty of jobs and internships to give her work experience – including an internship with the then senator for California, Alan Cranston. Neither of them knew that thirty years later, she would be the senator for California herself!

At Howard University, her friends and tutors noticed that she was good at arguing and debating – whether that was about politics, society or other things. There was a lot to debate in the 1980s, from nuclear weapons and the Cold War, to apartheid in South Africa. Like other Black students of her generation, Kamala felt a sense of responsibility to get a good education so she could change the world for the better.

TROUBLE IN THE 1980S

In the 1980s, while Kamala was at university, a few people in the USA – like Donald Trump – were making more money than ever through property and the stock market. Most of the world, however, had plenty to worry about.

The Cold War Since the 1950s, the USSR (modern-day Russia) and the USA had been rivals, with very different ways of thinking. Both were keen to control the world. Both tried to get as many nuclear weapons as possible, so that the other would not dare attack them. This deadly competition was called the nuclear arms race. During the 1980s everyone worried about a nuclear war. Children learned to hide at the sound of an alert that might mean a nuclear bomb was falling on them.

After Germany lost the Second World War, a wall had been built through the centre of its capital, Berlin, splitting it into two sections. East Berlin was controlled by the USSR. West Berlin followed the USA's ideas. On 9 November 1989, the wall began to be officially taken down. It was part of a wave of revolutions that ended the USSR and with it, the Cold War.

Apartheid In the 1980s, the USA might have been leaving segregation in the past, but in South Africa, segregation (called apartheid) was still a fact. People were segregated on the basis of their skin colour. Black people were kept out of good housing, health care and education. In the 1950s, Nelson Mandela had fought for the rights of Black South Africans, and had the support of many people all around the world. However, many European and American leaders called him a terrorist. Nelson Mandela had been in prison since 1962, but in the 1980s, protests against his imprisonment spread and grew. Finally, on 11 February 1990, just a few months after the fall of the Berlin Wall, Nelson Mandela was released from prison. He had been locked up for twenty-seven years, just for fighting for equality. Later he became the leader of South Africa; an incredible journey from prisoner to president.

Nelson Mandela

Back to the West Coast

After graduating from Howard University in 1986 with a degree in political science and economics, Kamala returned to California. Here, she started at law school, at the University of California, to train as an attorney. An attorney is a lawyer who is qualified to represent people in court. She became president of the Black Law Students' Association (BLSA). At the time, Black law students were finding it harder to get jobs than white ones, and so Kamala called the managing partners of all the law firms and asked them to send people to the BLSA's job fair. It was great practice in making changes happen, by picking up the phone and not being afraid to call powerful people and ask them to help. She would need to do a lot of that as a politician, asking for support for her campaigns!

It seemed that Kamala was doing what her family expected and wanted her to do: she was forging a career in a way that could help people as well as make the most of her talents. But there would soon be trouble, because her family had never expected that she would want to qualify as a prosecutor.

THURGOOD MARSHALL
(1908–1993)

Thurgood Marshall was an American lawyer and civil rights activist. He was born in Baltimore, Maryland. His mother was a teacher and his father was a railway porter. He went to study at the Howard School of Law. It took Thurgood some time to settle down to working hard, but when he did, he was a brilliant lawyer. He became involved with the National Association for the Advancement of Colored People (NAACP), an organization that fought for Black Americans' civil rights, often using the courts to get changes in the law.

In 1951, thirteen people, including a man called Oliver Brown, filed a complaint against the Board of Education in the US state of Kansas. Their children were being sent to school by bus miles from their homes, because local schools were not allowed to accept Black children. They, like many Black people in the USA, thought this was wrong. But the court in Kansas rejected their case. So the parents asked the NAACP to help.

Thurgood Marshall asked the Supreme Court, the most important court in the USA, to look at this judgment and think again. Thurgood argued in court that segregation was wrong in itself, even if the schools were of equal standard. Being kept apart from others on the basis of your skin colour was against the Constitution. In 1954, Thurgood won this famous case, which was known as Brown vs Board of Education. Slowly but surely, the victory led to all schools in the USA becoming desegregated.

In 1967, with the support of President Kennedy and President Johnson, Thurgood

Marshall was made a judge of the Supreme Court – the first Black American to hold this powerful position.

"THE LEGAL SYSTEM CAN FORCE OPEN DOORS, AND SOMETIMES EVEN KNOCK DOWN WALLS, BUT IT CANNOT BUILD BRIDGES. THAT JOB BELONGS TO YOU AND ME."

Thurgood Marshall, acceptance speech after receiving the Liberty Award, *NAACP Legal Defense and Educational Fund, Inc.* (1992)

CAREER PROSECUTOR

"Kamala Harris, for the People"

··

"AMERICA HAS A DEEP AND DARK HISTORY OF PEOPLE USING THE POWER OF THE PROSECUTOR AS AN INSTRUMENT OF INJUSTICE."

Kamala Harris, *The Truths We Hold* (2019)

In the USA, a defence attorney protects someone who has been accused of breaking the law. Prosecutors are the other side of the coin. They are lawyers who build and present a case against someone who is suspected of breaking the law. They look at the evidence to decide who should be charged with a crime and what crime they should be charged with (for example, whether to charge them with murder or the less serious crime of unintentional killing, called manslaughter). Prosecutors have to be good at making clear, convincing arguments, good at showing evidence for their opinions and expert at persuading people that their view is the right one. They have to have the confidence to stand up in court and be tough enough to go on the attack. They have to be up for a verbal fight, but self-controlled enough not to let their feelings overwhelm them.

Later in life, Kamala would refer to her training as a prosecutor when she said: "I have been trained, and my experience over decades, is to make decisions after a review of the evidence and the facts." She loved the fact that prosecutors did not represent a single person, but the whole of society. That was what she wanted to do. Every prosecutor begins arguing their case by speaking their name followed by the words "for the people", which echoes the beginning of the American Constitution: "We, the People..." In the USA a crime against one person is considered a crime against every person. That was something that spoke powerfully to Kamala's sense of justice.

The Power of the Prosecutor

Prosecutors have a lot of power. If they suspect a crime might have been commited, they can run an investigation – which means they can find out whether the law has been broken. They have an influence on whether someone who is guilty should go to prison or pay a fine. Prosecutors can even ask for a criminal to be sentenced to death.

Prosecutors can choose to be clever in the way they make a case. They can give immunity to witnesses and accused criminals – so people can tell what they know about a crime without being afraid they will be charged with a crime themselves. They can "plea bargain", which means they can agree to give someone a lighter sentence in return for their help catching other, more dangerous criminals. If you want to break up a criminal gang, for example, is it a good idea to punish the less powerful criminals harshly, or would it be better to let them off with a lighter sentence if they agree to give evidence against the ringleader? These are tough questions, and there may be no right answers. As a prosecutor, however, at least you get to decide on the answers instead of waiting for other people's decisions. A prosecutor can act, while a defence attorney is limited to reacting.

Choosing to be a prosecutor, not a defence lawyer, might have seemed like an odd decision for someone who wanted to protect vulnerable people in society. But that was not how Kamala saw it. She wanted to be a "progressive prosecutor" – someone who used their power with fairness, wisdom and experience. Someone who created safe places to live by preventing and reducing crime, not locking more people up. Someone who had the power to make things better. "When you are in charge you don't have to ask permission to do the right thing," she said, about her decision to become a prosecutor.

So, she knew what she wanted to be, and why. But how would her family feel about it?

CONSTANCE BAKER MOTLEY
(1921–2005)

Constance was one of Kamala Harris' heroes.
Like Shirley Chisholm, she was the child of
immigrants from the Carribbean. Her mother
was a domestic worker and her father was
a chef. She wanted to go to university but
could not afford it until a wealthy white man,
Clarence W Blakeslee, heard her giving a
speech and was so impressed that he decided
to pay her tuition fees.

After university, she became a lawyer working
for the NAACP, like Thurgood Marshall. She
was the first Black American woman to
argue a case – Meredith vs Fair – before the
US Supreme Court. Like Brown vs Board of
Education, this was a case about the right of
Black and white students to study together.
She argued for James Meredith to be the first

Black student to attend the University of Mississippi in 1962 – and won. Her strength and determination were an inspiration to Kamala Harris.

Later, she became the first Black American woman appointed to the federal judiciary. In 1964 she was elected to the New York State Senate, part of the local government, where she worked to get better housing for people who did not have much money.

Constance Motley

Changing the System

"YOU NEVER HAVE TO ASK ANYONE PERMISSION TO LEAD. WHEN YOU WANT TO LEAD, YOU LEAD."

Kamala Harris, speaking to a teenage girl
at a rally, (2020)

Kamala knew that her family would be shocked and worried by her decision to become a prosecutor. Black women faced racism and sexism in all walks of life, but as a prosecutor Kamala would really be on her own. Even in 2020, only 2.8 per cent of all US lawyers were Black women, and only 1 per cent of prosecutors were women of colour. In the 1980s the numbers were even lower. Kamala's family feared she was taking on a job that was hard enough at the best of times, but especially lonely and difficult for a Black woman. They were happy for her to be a lawyer, but they thought she should become a defence attorney, not a prosecutor.

Kamala's family, community and friends saw every day that the law was a system that rarely actually delivered justice. Too often, the prosecutor was part of the injustice. Prosecutors would push for a prison sentence even for small, non-violent crimes when the criminal was Black. Police were often racist and would assume that Black people were dangerous even when they were not. Judges would give Black people unfairly heavy sentences. To Black Americans, it seemed as if the people in power did not care about their lives.

But here, as always, Kamala knew exactly what she wanted to be doing and why. She knew that prosecutors had done bad things, but she also knew some had gone after corrupt politicians, rich businesses who didn't care if they poisoned drinking water as long as they made money, and white supremacist terrorist groups like the Ku Klux Klan. Created in 1865, as a result of the abolishment of slavery in America, the Ku Klux Klan formed to continue to spread their racist beliefs. Although American society had moved forward since 1865, there was were a lot of people who were racist and this often impacted how Black people were convicted of crimes. She wanted to be a "progressive prosecutor", someone who worked from inside the system to fix justice so it was really justice, and protected victims by making criminals account for their crimes. In her words, "I went into the system to change it." Eventually her family came round to her point of view.

Learning to Fail

Kamala started her journey to being a prosecutor by interning at the Alameda District Attorney's Office – one of only two women to do so at the time. The district attorney was the lawyer in charge of prosecuting all the crimes in the local area (in this case, Alameda County). The district attorney had a staff of many deputy district attorneys working in his office, who handled less important cases. Once they had interned and passed the bar exam – an exam testing her knowledge and skills as a lawyer – Kamala and the other interns hoped to be offered a job as a deputy district attorney.

Right from the start, it was exciting. Kamala got to be part of a team collecting evidence and building strong cases against criminals, who had done anything from driving under the influence of alcohol, to murder. She got to see how the criminal justice system worked and how she could make a difference. Once, she was able to help a woman who had been arrested simply for being at the scene of a crime. Kamala made sure her case was heard quickly and the woman was released without having to spend a night in prison. To Kamala, this was a life-changing experience that proved "how much it mattered to have compassionate people working as prosecutors".

At the end of her internship, Kamala was overjoyed to be offered a job as a deputy district attorney for Alameda County. All she needed to do to start her career was finish her third year of studying and pass her bar exam. That was where it all came unstuck. In 1989, she took her bar exam – and failed.

It was a shock to Kamala. She felt embarrassed, humiliated and upset, but she also knew she had to step up and fix things. She had to retake the exam, and pass this time. Luckily the job was going to be kept open for her, but she had to get used to going into the office and seeing the other interns move on with their training, and also get used to people's disappointment in her. She had to be resilient, and not quit. She passed on the second attempt.

WHAT IS PROGRESSIVE PROSECUTION?

As Kamala's family had pointed out to her, prosecutors do not have a reputation as kind, compassionate people. However, it all depends on the prosecutor! There are over two thousand prosecutors in the USA. A Harvard Law School review in 2016 showed that just five of them were responsible for most of the death sentences handed out in the USA between 1974 and 2015. This included the execution of a sixteen-year-old with a mental health disorder, which horrified human rights organizations across the world. (In 2005 the US Supreme Court banned the execution of under eighteens.)

But there is a new movement among prosecutors like Kamala Harris, to change the system from the inside. It has more and more support in the USA from voters. These "progressive prosecutors" aim to prevent crime before they punish it. They believe that the current system doesn't work to keep people safe. Instead, it makes criminals of people who are simply poor, or have mental health problems, and who are often people of colour. Progressive prosecutors like Kamala Harris often support:

• finding other solutions than prison to non-violent crime

- abolishing the death penalty

- acting against wrongful convictions and abuse of powers by the police

- ending the cash bail system for less serious crimes (see page 92).

When Justice Isn't Fair

Finally a qualified prosecutor, Kamala Harris was on her own. Now she had the huge responsibility of prosecuting someone in court; standing up in front of the court and showing them that her opinions were well-founded and should convince them. She had to ask the right questions in cross-examination, and show the court she was a trustworthy prosecutor. It was not something you could prepare for through lectures or reading, it was something you had to learn by living it. The workload was heavy: she would be dealing with over a hundred cases at once, and she had to keep the details straight so that she did not get confused in court.

It was hard work emotionally, too. She was working on violent cases like murders and could be called in the middle of the night to get to a crime scene where someone lay dead. Then she had to make sure the evidence was collected. Even though she knew that someone had committed a crime, she still had to be able to prove it in court or the criminal would walk free. A particularly difficult but important part of her job was working on crimes against children – prosecuting those who had hurt them. It brought back memories of her school friend from Montreal, who had come to stay with them for her safety when her stepfather had hurt her. Many years later in her vice presidential acceptance speech, Kamala would say one of the reasons she had wanted to become a prosecutor was to help people like her friend.

Sometimes, Kamala had to face the fact that although both she and the victim knew what had happened, they would not be able to get evidence to prove it in front of the court. And sometimes, the court did not care or want to listen, even when there was evidence. Kamala knew that everyone deserved justice, whether they were likeable or not. Justice should not depend on whether the people in the jury box thought the victim was "their kind of person" or not. Especially not when the victim was a child. Yet too often, that was what happened. The law did not always lead to justice. It was something that Kamala hated, and throughout her career she would try to make juries see that everyone deserved justice.

Going to San Francisco

In 1998, Kamala was offered a promotion, which would mean moving from Alameda County to the San Francisco District Attorney's Office. The San Francisco District Attorney was Terence Hallinan, a lawyer with a messy past, who used to be a boxer and still tended to punch people when he got angry. It was never going to be an easy job, but as a prosecutor, Kamala was not afraid of conflict. Besides, she and Hallinan agreed on many things. They both had progressive approaches to prosecution – they believed that crime could not be stopped just by punishing criminals harshly, you had to stop the things that caused crime, like poverty. Hallinan himself had a criminal record so he knew about the law from both sides.

Office seal

Kamala was put in charge of the career criminal unit, which was focused on prosecuting violent and serial offenders. It was the kind of challenge she loved, but as it turned out, she had not realized just how difficult it would be to make a success of it. Hallinan's office turned out to be a chaotic, unhappy place to work. People were angry and upset and didn't work as a team. Sometimes, people were fired without warning. There was no organization, and – worst of all – the disorganization meant that victims of crime didn't get justice. The office was like a machine that was broken, and the new job quickly felt like a trap. After eighteen months, Kamala was glad to be offered another job, in the San Francisco City Attorney's Office.

Although the San Francisco District Attorney and the San Francisco City Attorney sound very similar, they are very different jobs – while the San Francisco District Attorney is in charge of prosecuting crime in the district of San Francisco, the San Francisco City Attorney works for the Mayor of San Francisco. The San Francisco City Attorney asked Kamala Harris to lead their Child and Family Services department. Kamala agreed, but she did not want to feel trapped as she had done before in the District Attorney's Office. She made it a condition of accepting the job that she would be allowed to make improvements. Feeling powerless to change things for the better was a horrible feeling that she never wanted to have again.

Kamala was always really interested in how people's childhoods affected their lives. She had been lucky to have a loving family and a great nursery teacher in Mrs Shelton, but not everyone was so lucky. As a prosecutor she often met people who'd had terrible childhoods, full of neglect and cruelty. Some of these people went on to be in juvenile detention (a prison-like facility for people under eighteen years old), and later, ended up being arrested and imprisoned as adults. Kamala believed that far too often someone who had been hurt as a child went on to hurt others, not because they were bad, but because that was all they had learned. It wasn't fair; people were put on a conveyor belt they could not escape, because of their circumstances. She wanted to change that.

In the City Attorney's Office, she set up a

group to study the problems facing young people who, like her friend in Montreal, had been abused. She worked with people who had suffered abuse, and with communities to come up with a plan to try and stop things getting even worse for these victims. Often these children had no one to turn to, so the group created a safe place in the city that would be there for them, offering support. The plan worked, and Kamala began to think about what she could do next to improve things.

In many places in the USA, voters get to choose their district attorney in an election. San Francisco was one of these cities, and an election was coming up. There had never been a Black, female District Attorney of San Francisco before. But Kamala had plenty of ideas, she wasn't afraid of a challenge, and she had proved through her work at the City Attorney's Office that she could turn her ideas into change that really helped people. If Terence Hallinan wasn't doing a good job as district attorney, maybe she could give voters in San Francisco the chance to choose her instead?

WHAT IS A POLITICAL PARTY?

A political party is an organization that chooses candidates to stand for election to help run the country. Members of a political party may have similar ideas about how society should work, although within big political parties, there are usually many different points of view.

Political parties active today include: the Republican Party (USA), the Democratic Party (USA), the Conservative Party (UK), the Labour Party (UK), the Green Party (UK), the African National Congress (South Africa) and Bharatiya Janata (India).

Political parties are supposed to be a part of a democratic system, meaning that each citizen can choose which party they support. However, sometimes people are forced to be members of a political party. For example, the National Socialist party in 1930s Germany was led by Adolf Hitler, a dictator (a ruler who keeps control by force). Germans who did not join the Nazi party were bullied, discriminated against and imprisoned.

KAMALA HARRIS
FOR CALIFORNIA

"A Voice for Justice"

"I ALWAYS START MY CAMPAIGNS EARLY, AND I RUN HARD. MAYBE IT COMES FROM THE ROUGH-AND-TUMBLE WORLD OF SAN FRANCISCO POLITICS, WHERE IT'S NOT EVEN A CONTACT SPORT — IT'S A BLOOD SPORT."

Kamala Harris, in an interview with
The New York Times (2015)

Kamala's friends and colleagues already believed in her and thought she could do a good job. But campaigning to be elected district attorney meant she needed more than friends to support her – she needed a whole team of people, including strangers. Being elected was not as simple as being the best person for the job, you had to be the most popular. People had to believe in you. In order to believe in you, they had to hear about you. Kamala would need volunteers to walk along streets and knock on doors, singing her praises to people. She would need money to pay for advertisements and staff to work on her campaign. She had to set up an office and show everyone what she was about – it would be a full-time job just trying to get elected to do the full-time job!

There were many wealthy areas in San Francisco, where people had money to give to their favourite politician to help them campaign. The Bayview was not one of these areas. It was a poor area of San Francisco, where people had a hard time making a living and achieving their dreams, but that was where Kamala decided to base her campaign. These were the people who didn't get much out of the justice system, and these were the people she wanted to help.

"It was places like the Bayview that inspired me to run in the first place," she said in her memoir. She was going to be fighting for people like those who lived in the Bayview, to make their local streets safer, not just the streets where rich people lived. Setting up her campaign headquarters there was a powerful statement of what she was all about.

Now Kamala also needed to go out and convince people to vote for her. After being a prosecutor, how hard could it be? But she was not going to be in court here, trying to convince a judge and jury with strict rules in place and the ability to go home at the end of the day. She herself was on trial – with the voters as judge and jury. She went out to busy supermarkets and shopping centres and set up an ironing board as a standing desk, with a sign taped to it: KAMALA HARRIS: A VOICE FOR JUSTICE. Her family and friends helped get the word out. It took a lot of determination and strength of character. She had to take rejection from angry people, people who disagreed with her and people who just did not want to be badgered by a politician. She had to try to get complete strangers to think that they should be voting for her.

Public approval – being liked – wasn't part of being a prosecutor in court, but now Kamala had to poll people, to find out what they thought of her policies, and if they liked her as a person enough to vote for her. At first, most people hadn't even heard of her let alone decided whether they liked her or not. The big challenge, especially in a big district like San Francisco, is getting people to know who you are. When she began campaigning, only six per cent of people had heard of her. Terence Hallinan, however, was much better known because he was already in the job. Why would people trust her to do a better job?

In fact, her support was growing over time. In 2004, after a tough political battle, Kamala became the elected district attorney of San Francisco, beating her opponent, with 56 per cent of the vote. She gave her victory speech in front of a graffiti-covered wall at her campaign headquarters in the Bayview. Speaking to her supporters, she promised to make the District

Attorney's Office into somewhere they could be proud of. She was not going to make voters choose between progressive, compassionate treatment of criminals, and justice for victims. She was going to make sure that they got both. Wishing her luck as he accepted his defeat, Terence Hallinan commented: "It's a tough job." There was no doubt about that!

Kamala's win made her the first woman and Afro-Indian district attorney in the whole of California. Kamala inherited an empty office with a twenty-year-old computer and a chair, but it was a starting point – the starting point for change.

A Tough Job

As a prosecutor, Kamala Harris was used to being disliked, even hated. As a politician, she was used to being criticized by her opponent. But when your decision can't help but hurt people, whatever path you choose, and when people you respect don't agree with your decision, it's a different matter. The thing about wanting to be the one who makes the tough, important decisions is that you also have to be the one who takes the responsibility when people think you made a really bad decision. This huge challenge came soon after she had been elected District Attorney of San Francisco in 2004.

A few months after Kamala's election, a twenty-nine-year-old police officer, Isaac Espinoza, was shot and killed in the Bayview, the very place where Kamala had set up her campaign. Isaac was a popular police officer who cared a lot about helping people and was good at calming down violent situations. The person who shot him, David Hill, was twenty-one years old. David Hill had a hard life from childhood, and had eventually joined a gang. Isaac Espinoza was shot with fourteen rounds from an assault rifle. He had not been wearing uniform at the time – in other words, it was not necessarily clear to David Hill that Isaac Espinoza, who was chasing him on foot when he was shot, was a policeman on duty. These were just some of the facts that the prosecutor had to think about when deciding what punishment to ask the court to hand down to David Hill. For killing an officer on duty, he could easily face the death penalty.

One thing that Kamala had promised voters in her campaign was that she would never seek the death penalty. She did not think it helped to stop crime, and did not think it was morally right. Most voters in San Francisco agreed with her. Others however, disagreed. A lot of voters wanted the death penalty in this case. This police officer had been young, with a wife and children, and had tried hard to help people. He was a "good cop". They wanted his killer to pay for what he had done. Many people also argued that the death penalty would put off others from killing, and that this was the time to use it.

THE DEATH PENALTY IN THE USA

Should a criminal ever be put to death for their crimes? Across the UK, the death penalty was abolished in 1973. But in the USA, it is still a legal penalty in twenty-seven states. It is reserved for the most extreme crimes, and it can take years for a sentence of death to turn into an actual execution. This wait for execution is known as being "on death row".

Death is a legal penalty in many other countries across the world, not just the USA. Internationally, people are put to death for things that would not be considered crimes in the UK or USA, such as saying bad things about the state religion.

Sticking to Your Values

It was Kamala's decision whether or not to call for the death penalty. She would have to face the consequences of her decision. She stuck to her own values and to the promise she had made to voters, and decided not to seek the death penalty for David Hill. Many of her most influential supporters were furious, and so were the police, who felt that they were not defended in their difficult and dangerous job. This was a headache for Kamala, because as chief prosecutor, she was the leader of the police and responsible for looking after them.

police badge

At Isaac Espinoza's funeral, which was packed with his police colleagues, another Democratic politician, Dianne Feinstein spoke against Kamala's decision not to go for the death penalty. Dianne was a legendary politician who had broken many barriers – the first woman to be mayor of San Francisco and the first woman from California to serve in the Senate. She had helped to introduce laws on issues that Kamala also cared about passionately, such as stopping gun violence, protecting immigrant children and protecting the environment. Now this widely respected woman was calling Kamala out, saying that she had made the wrong decision. Thousands of people stood up and cheered the speech. Kamala was also at the funeral, and she had to face the consequences of her decision in a horribly public way.

Was hers the wrong decision or was it the right one? That depended on your point of view. But one thing was clear as time went on, which was that Kamala stuck to her principles – and the promise she had made to voters – even when it was very, very difficult to do so. Being in the system, having power to change things, also meant being the obvious person to blame when anything went wrong. It was a test of whether she was tough enough for the position she had been voted into, and if she could be tough enough for all the other challenges she would certainly face if she continued in politics. To most people's minds, she passed the toughness test – not because she necessarily made the right decision, but because she made a hard decision and accepted responsibility for it.

The Prison Problem

There are some big questions that every lawyer has to think about in their career. For example, what is prison for? How should we prevent crime? What should be done with criminals and why? In particular, do we send criminals to prison as a punishment or revenge, to "teach them a lesson"? Or is it for keeping others safe from criminals? And when people are in prison, what is prison meant to do? Is it supposed to deter criminals from committing crime? Or is it a place where criminals should be rehabilitated – learn how to be law-abiding people and get support to stop them from committing crimes again?

During her time as District Attorney of San Francisco, one of the things Kamala knew she had to do was reduce the number of people who went to prison. When she became district attorney, the prisons in California were hugely overcrowded – so much so that they were not safe places to be. In an overcrowded prison, prisoners could not be kept safe.

The popular "tough on crime" approach, suggested that sending criminals to prison would protect law-abiding people, and would also teach the criminal a lesson. Surely after they were released they would never again break the law for fear of being sent back to prison. In fact, things didn't seem to work out that way. Across the USA, millions of people were in prison, even when they had only committed a small crime, and far too many of them kept coming back to prison once they were released. How could this problem be solved?

CASH BAIL SYSTEM

One reason for the many people in prison is the cash bail system. Sometimes when someone is arrested, they are allowed to leave prison and go on with their lives while they wait for trial. However, this is only if they can pay a fee to the court, called a cash bail bond. The average bond is $10,000, but most people don't have enough savings to pay this. People without $10,000 dollars spare have to stay in prison waiting for a trial, unless they plead guilty. Is that really fair? Some people plead guilty even if they are innocent, just to get out of prison and continue with their jobs so they can pay the rent and get their children to school.

Back on Track

Kamala, from her experience as a prosecutor, had learned that prison was not the right solution for every crime. Often, it made things worse. She had seen children grow up in areas where crime and violence were all around them; where they felt they had to carry a weapon to defend themselves. They had only ever known violence, abuse and instability. Was it any surprise that they ended up committing a crime? Other people might be sent to prison for a non-violent crime, but when in prison, become influenced by much worse criminals and not get any help to change. When they came out of prison, their criminal record stopped them getting a job. So to get some money to survive, they might go and commit more crimes.

There were many other reasons that the system needed reform. Lawyers were just as likely to have prejudices as anyone, and so sometimes people got a harsh sentence just because of how they dressed, where they lived or what music they had on in their car. Then, thrown into the prison system, they could never get out again – it was like a hamster wheel or a revolving door, a trap that people couldn't escape. Kamala wanted to help all the victims, including the ones who were the victims of the broken justice system.

PREJUDICE, UNCONSCIOUS BIAS AND DISCRIMINATION

Have you ever looked at a food and decided you won't like it, just because of the way it looks? Maybe years later you try it and discover it's delicious! That is a **prejudice**. A prejudice is an unfair belief that someone holds, that is not based on evidence or good reasoning. When it comes to food it doesn't matter much, but it does matter when it comes to people. It is even worse if a lawyer or policeman has a prejudice against a person. For example, a judge might believe that everyone from a certain neighbourhood is a criminal. If you came from that neighbourhood, they might well judge you guilty of a crime even if you are really innocent. Some prejudices are so widespread that they have their own name, like racism, antisemitism (prejudice against Jews) or transphobia (prejudice against transgender people).

Unconscious biases are the prejudices we don't even know we have. We all learn, before we can even think about it, to prefer people who look like our family. That is natural but if, when we go to school or work, we are suspicious of everyone who looks a bit different from us, we can end up discriminating against them.

Discrimination is when a prejudice ends up making us treat one group of people worse than another. For example, if a girl doesn't get picked for a football team because the captain doesn't believe that girls can play football, it really matters because it isn't fair. When Martin Luther King Jr, the famous civil rights leader, said, "I have a dream that my four little children will one day live in a nation where they will not be judged by the colour of their skin but by the content of their character," he was asking for an end to prejudice and discrimination in the USA.

Dr Martin Luther King Jr

Kamala's plan to solve the problem of prisons was called the "Back on Track" programme. The idea behind it was to get people into legal employment instead of putting them in prison. She changed things so that people who had been convicted of a less serious, non-violent crime were offered a choice. They could go to prison, or they could join the Back on Track programme. Back on Track gave these people a lot of help to change their lives, from finding them a job to getting them counselling, and from sending them to parenting classes to making sure they had health checks. It gave them whatever they needed to get away from the bad influences in their lives. It also demanded a lot from them. To get on to the programme, they had to plead guilty and accept their sentence, find a job or continue their education, and complete community service. If they did everything they were asked to, their criminal record would be wiped clean. It was hard work, but they were back on track to a good future, not trapped in the prison system.

The programme was a big success. After two years, only 10 per cent of Back on Track graduates had re-offended, compared to 50 per cent of others who had gone to prison for similar crimes. The Back on Track programme was also much, much cheaper than prosecuting people and housing them in prison. It was so effective that in 2009, when Barack Obama became president, his government took it on and made it the model for a nationwide programme.

It was no coincidence that it was also in 2009 that Kamala wrote a book about her views on making a safer country, called *Smart on Crime: A Career Prosecutor's Plan to Make Us Safe*. She said that instead of choosing between being "tough on crime" (punishing even tiny crimes severely) and being "soft on crime" (not punishing criminals at all), it was better to be "smart on crime". That meant punishing violent crimes severely, but also looking at what caused crime, and trying to stop those causes. The book was a way of getting her ideas out to a much wider audience – not just other lawyers and politicians, but voters across the country. It signalled to everyone that she wanted her ideas and influence to spread much further than just San Francisco. She decided the time was right to seek election for an even more important job: Attorney General of California.

Taking Charge of California:
Attorney General of California:
2011-2017

Each state in the USA has an attorney general who is in charge of the many district attorneys. Kamala knew that being California's attorney general would let her bring Back on Track to the whole of the state. But more than that, her influence would spread much further than the state itself. She would be working with other attorney generals on nationwide crimes – an exciting, inspiring thought.

For her other elections, she hadn't needed to stand for a political party. But for this important position, she had to be selected and supported by a political party. She already knew that she would represent the Democratic Party – it was the party that had the policies she believed in, and that her heroes such as Shirley Chisholm and Thurgood Marshall had belonged to. It was also the party of the person who had in 2009 broken down the biggest barrier by becoming the USA's first Black President – Barack Hussein Obama II.

She was excited to plan her campaign and gather her staff together, and she was hopeful that she would win. But then bad news hit her and her family.

PRESIDENT BARACK HUSSEIN OBAMA II

Barack Obama was the forty-forth president of the USA. He was born in Hawaii to an American mother and a father from Kenya. Like Kamala his parents had divorced. His father was killed in a car crash in 1982. He grew up with his mother and stepfather in Indonesia and in Honolulu. He is married to Michelle and they have two daughters, Malia and Sasha.

Barack Obama went to Columbia and Harvard universities, and like Kamala, became an attorney, working in Chicago, Illinois.

A Democract, he was elected to the Illinois State Senate, and then to the United States Senate. In 2007 the Democrats chose him above Hillary Clinton to be their presidential candidate, and he in turn chose Joe Biden as the person he wanted for his vice president. In November 2008 Barack Obama was elected president of the USA, making him the country's first Black president. He was in office until 2017. His most important achievement during his presidency is often said to be making health care affordable for more people across the USA through the Patient Protection and Affordable Care Act.

Kamala's beloved mother, Shyamala, was suffering from cancer. As the months passed, she became more and more unwell. The same year that Barack Obama became the USA's first Black president, with Joe Biden as his vice president, Shyamala Gopalan Harris died. It was a huge loss for Kamala and her sister Maya. Their mother had been a powerful inspiration and role model for them throughout their lives. She had been Kamala's biggest supporter as she ran for election as District Attorney of San Francisco, always at her side to support her and cheer her on.

SHYAMALA GOPALAN HARRIS (1938-2009)

Born into a Brahmin family who lived in a village in Tamil Nadu, India, Shyamala was the eldest of four children. She was a talented singer and musician in her teenage years, and was awarded her undergraduate degree from Delhi University at the age of nineteen. Although no one from her family had ever been to the USA, she set off, alone, to study for a PhD in nutrition and endocrinology from Berkeley University. Nutrition is the science of how food affects your body, and endocrinology is the science of hormones (chemicals in the body that change behaviour). During her PhD she became involved in the civil rights movement and met Donald Harris, Kamala's father. She brought her daughters up to be confident, ambitious and to help others.

Shyamala, Maya and Kamala

After her divorce from Donald, she began working as a researcher at Berkeley University. She was interested in how hormones affected breast cancer. In Montreal, she continued her research at McGill University. Throughout her life she made many discoveries, which helped people understand how breast cancer happens and what could be done to prevent and cure it. She also never stopped helping others and caring about justice. She made sure that many young people got the help they needed to start a career in science and medical research.

California was a huge state with an enormous population of 39 million. Its attorney general represented and worked for all of those 39 million people, to make sure they got justice and were kept safe. So, if you wanted people to vote for you, you had to start by telling those 39 million people who you were and what you could do for them. You had to show them you were the right person for this highly important job with all its responsibility. That took more money, more organization and more campaigning than Kamala had ever done before. Kamala spent many days and nights simply travelling around the state, meeting people, speaking to them and trying to persuade them that she was the person who could keep them safe. It was a whirlwind, exhausting tour.

One of her big breakthroughs came when she was mentioned on *Tonight with David Letterman* – a television programme that was very popular all across the USA. A guest who had written a book about Black leaders called Kamala Harris brilliant and smart, and compared her to the new president, Barack Obama. The media jumped on it, and she got lots of attention, including being named one of *Newsweek* magazine's most powerful women. It was great to be interviewed on TV and radio and for the whole country to know who she was and what her ideas about stopping crime were. Her confidence, honesty and sense of humour won a lot of people over.

Proposition 8

Meanwhile, the Republicans – the other big political party – were backing the experienced

Steve Cooley, District Attorney of Los Angeles, for the job. The Republican Party put a lot of money into trying to defeat Kamala. Voters had not forgotten the murder of Isaac Espinoza in 2004 and the fact that Kamala had not called for the death penalty for his murderer. The Republicans paid for advertisements that reminded voters of that. In return, Kamala reminded voters that her rival's record on environmental crime was poor, and told voters that she would stop the revolving door of the prison system, with the help of programmes like Back on Track.

Above all, however, "Proposition 8" was the big difference between the two candidates. Throughout her career, Kamala Harris had stood up for LGBTQ+ rights in many ways. She had created a Hate Crimes Unit that would look into hate crimes against LGBTQ+ teenagers in schools. She had fought against the so-called "gay and trans panic defence", which made it acceptable for people to try and excuse their murder of others because their victims were gay or trans. San Francisco had long had a reputation as being welcoming to LGBTQ+ people, but the rest of California was not always as positive. Proposition 8 was evidence of this.

In California, voters were allowed to propose laws, which the attorney general had to spend time discussing. In California, people of the same sex had been allowed to get married. But in 2008, the people of California proposed to change the law, so that only marriage between one man and one woman was allowed. This was called Proposition 8. As District Attorney of San Francisco, Kamala flatly refused to support this proposition. She thought that everybody should have the right to marry, whether they loved someone of the same or the opposite sex. She went on to argue that the only people with any "standing" or right to be heard on whether this law should be passed or not, were same-sex couples who wanted to marry. For others, it was none of their business. It was not okay to prevent others from marrying just because you didn't personally agree with it. Her winning argument eventually led to the Supreme Court of the USA deciding that same-sex couples had the same right to marry as anyone else and making that a law across the whole USA in 2015.

But in 2009, when Kamala Harris was campaigning to be attorney general for the whole of California, that Supreme Court decision was a long way away. Kamala told voters that she would continue to fight against Proposition 8. Her rival, Steve Cooley, told everyone that he would support Proposition 8. The question was, who would Californians side with?

PROTECTING LGBTQ+ PEOPLE

The LGBTQ+ acronym stands for lesbian, gay, bisexual, transgender and queer. The + stands for the many other gender identities that people have. Throughout modern history, people who are attracted to others of the same sex, or whose gender is different from the one they were assigned at birth, have been discriminated against. For example, they have not been allowed to marry who they want to, or serve in the military. Often, people are attacked, harassed and bullied because they are, or are believed to be, LGBTQ+. When someone is attacked because of who they are or are believed to be, this is called a hate crime. It is different from other crimes because the attacker is motivated by hatred of a specific group (for example, gay people, or Muslims). Hate crimes can be motivated by hatred of a race, religion, sexual orientation, disability, or because the victim is transgender.

A Win – Just About!

Election night came, and it was tense and nerve-wracking. As she watched the news reports as the votes came in, it became clear to Kamala that it was a tight race between her and Steve Cooley. As soon as it looked as if one person was sure to get a majority, the news would make an announcement. When the announcement came, it was a win for Steve Cooley. The next morning the San Francisco Chronicle printed a headline that Steve Cooley had won. It was a crushing disappointment. But it turned out that they had spoken a little too soon.

With more than nine million votes cast, across the third-largest state in the USA, getting the numbers right was not a simple or quick job. A few nail-biting weeks passed as more votes were counted. Then, three weeks later, Steve Cooley called Kamala. She was getting on to a plane and took his phone call just before she had to switch her phone off for take off. He was calling to concede. He had lost. All the votes were in and she had won by a tiny margin – less than one per cent of the vote.

It was still a win. She was now attorney general for the most populous state in the USA – as many people lived in California as lived in many countries around the world. She would have a budget of millions, a staff of 5,000 people, but also be responsible for a prison system containing over 135,000 inmates of which 750 were awaiting execution on death row. There was a lot of work to do – but it started with something joyful: letting everyone know that same sex couples could get married once again.

Attorney General Achievements

One of the things that Kamala was proudest of achieving as Attorney General of California was getting a better compensation deal for people who had lost their houses following the financial crisis in 2008. She had seen how proud her mother was of having bought their own house. It was an important part of the "American Dream", which promised immigrants to the USA that if they just worked hard enough, life could be better for their children. They would have a home they owned and could be secure in. That was the promise, but the reality was different. Since 2001, banks had been lending money to buy houses to people who could not really afford to pay it back. Then, in 2008, the global financial crisis happened.

FINANCIAL CRISIS OF 2007–2008

You might think of a bank as a place where you put your money to keep it safe. Usually, that is true. However, did you know that banks make money by lending people money – the same money that you put in there? When people borrow money from banks, such as a mortgage to buy a home, they have to pay back more than they borrow (this is called interest).

When millions of people do this, it adds up to a lot of extra money for the banks! But the banks rely on people being able to pay back what they owe. Banks are supposed to carry out checks to see if the people they are lending money to can afford to pay it back. But in the early 2000s, the banks were giving out too many mortgages to people who could not afford to pay it back. When too many people were unable to pay back their mortgages, the banks ran out of money. In the end, this affected the whole planet, and banks in other countries ran out of money too. People could not get money out of the banks to pay their bills, families were made homeless and whole countries could not pay their debts. Governments like the UK and the USA had to "bail out the banks", or take tens of billions of their currency out of the country to pay the banks' debts for them so they did not go bankrupt.

It was one of the worst financial crises in history, and the world as a whole became around two trillion dollars poorer as a result of it. The world is still suffering from the effects of the crisis, and people are poorer today than they would have been if it had not happened.

Beating the Banks

In California alone, millions of people lost their jobs during the financial crisis and could not pay their mortgages back. Banks foreclosed – claimed back the houses they had lent money on – and people lost their homes. Children were made homeless through no fault of their own. Pets were abandoned when people left their homes and had nowhere to keep them. It was devastating for many communities across California and the rest of the USA.

Even worse, some newspapers reported that people had had their mortgage foreclosed even though they didn't owe as much as the banks said they did. When the Attorney General's Office looked into it, they found that the banks, scrabbling to get back money they should never have lent out in the first place, had been making people homeless with no justification. It turned out that the systems being used to decide if someone owed a lot of money were badly flawed. Banks had been illegally taking away people's homes for years.

At the heart of the financial crisis was the question of whether the banks had broken the law. As attorney general, Kamala joined in a massive, national legal investigation into the banks' actions. The banks had broken their own rules by lending to people they should never have lent to, and both she and the other Attorney Generals from other states wanted to be sure that the banks would pay compensation to those people. It was especially important to her because Californian people – the people she represented – had been very badly affected.

The banks started off by offering a low sum of money to people who had lost their houses. Kamala rejected this at once. She and the other attorney generals fought until 2012, when the banks finally agreed to pay a much larger sum of money to people who had lost their homes unfairly. This was called the National Mortgage Settlement. She also drew up a document called the California Homeowners' Bill of Rights, with the aim of making laws to defend people against banks foreclosing on their homes in the future.

Not Enough Change

Throughout Kamala's life, things seemed in many ways to get better for Black Americans. In 2009, Barack Obama had become the first Black president. That was a barrier that many had not imagined could be overcome. Kamala, a Black woman, was now the top prosecutor for the most populous state in the USA.

And yet, although her achievements as a Black woman in the USA were extraordinary, she was often the first, or the only, Black or female person in the room. And despite the Obama presidency, it still seemed far too easy for white people, especially police, to kill Black people and get away with it. When Kamala had set out to be a prosecutor, back in the 1980s, her family had known the justice system was often biased against Black people. Things had changed, but not enough.

In 2012, Black teenager Trayvon Martin was shot. He was walking through Sanford, Florida, when George Zimmerman, a Hispanic American, saw him and reported him to the police for "acting suspiciously". Zimmerman then approached

Martin, and after a struggle, shot him dead. Zimmerman claimed he acted in self-defence and was not even charged with a crime by police. The injustice shocked people across the USA and the world. It took protests and pressure before Zimmerman was charged with a crime, and even then, he was allowed to walk free by the court with no consequences for killing someone.

This injustice, on top of many others, led to the beginning of the Black Lives Matter movement, boosted by social media into a worldwide campaign. In some ways the struggle for civil rights was still an ongoing battle, just as it had been when Kamala's parents were marching in the 1960s.

BLACK LIVES MATTER

When Trayvon Martin's killer was allowed to go free, to many people it seemed like a message that in the USA, Black lives did not matter. As a response, three Black women activists, Opal Tometti, Patrisse Cullors and Alicia Garza, began using the hashtag #BlackLivesMatter on social media. It developed into a powerful movement. Following the murder of George Floyd, by a white policeman in 2020, it inspired protests not just across the USA but across the world.

"#BLACKLIVESMATTER DOESN'T MEAN YOUR LIFE ISN'T IMPORTANT — IT MEANS THAT BLACK LIVES, WHICH ARE SEEN AS WITHOUT VALUE WITHIN WHITE SUPREMACY, ARE IMPORTANT TO YOUR LIBERATION."

Alicia Garza, *A Herstory of the #BlackLivesMatter Movement, The Feminist Wire* (2014)

Black Lives Matter protest

While Black Lives Matter has brought worldwide attention to the problem of police brutality against Black people, Kamala Harris is aware that it is not a new problem. As attorney general, Kamala Harris brought in unconscious bias education for the police who worked directly for her. We all have unconscious biases. But when the police are armed with guns, as they are in the USA, it is something that can make the difference between life and death. Police must be aware of when they might be making a decision to shoot based on their biases instead of for good reasons. However, some people have criticized Kamala for not speaking out more against police brutality during the Black Lives Matter protests.

Being a top prosecutor and a Black woman is a difficult balancing act. While many people thought she wasn't tough enough on crime, others thought she was too tough and had brought too many people into the broken prison system. One of her more controversial actions was making parents responsible for getting their children to school. This came out of her belief in the importance of early childhood education. She strongly believed that skipping school harmed children's lives, causing them to get caught up in crime and lose out on the education that would help them to get a job. So, she brought in a law making it a crime for parents not to make sure their children were getting an education. If pupils were enrolled in a school, they had to show up, or the parents could be sent to prison. Many people thought this was unfair on the parents. Later in her career, Kamala apologized to anyone who was hurt by the law.

Momala: Different Sorts of Families

"NOTHING I HAVE EVER ACCOMPLISHED COULD HAVE BEEN DONE ON MY OWN."

Kamala Harris, *The Truths We Hold* (2019)

Kamala's career as an elected prosecutor and politician, from district attorney to vice president of the USA, was not something that a single person could ever manage to achieve alone. There was a whole team working for her and trying to get her elected. Her sister and parents supported her throughout. The people who worked on her election campaigns also came to feel like family. However, finding a real-life family outside of work was more difficult.

With a busy, demanding career in one of the most difficult areas of law, and a total commitment to public service, it was always going to be hard for Kamala to find time to meet someone and make a family. Besides, experience had taught Kamala that as a woman in the public eye, people were going to be curious about who she dated – more than they would be if she were a man. It wasn't fair, it was sexist, and that was what she was trying to change – but if people got fixated on her love life instead of on her work, she would never have the chance to change anything. Any person she got together with would have to fit around her work, and not every person was willing to do that. Dating always had to come last. So it was not until she was Attorney General of California that a "blind date" turned into something more. Her friend arranged for her to go on a date with a stranger, sure that the two of them would get on.

WHO WORKS ON AN ELECTION CAMPAIGN?

If you're interested in politics, but you don't want to be the one trying to get elected (the candidate), there are still lots of ways to get involved in the US election system.

The **field department** gets in touch with voters to try and encourage them to vote for the candidate. They organize events, phone people up and knock on doors to tell them about how great the candidate is.

The **communications department** organizes advertisements and press releases. They make sure that everyone hears the right message about the candidate. They might set up interviews with TV channels or newspapers, and be ready with a quick answer when the other parties attack their candidate.

The **fundraising department** makes sure that the election campaign has all the money it needs to run. Travelling around the country making speeches is not cheap! In the 2020 US elections, the candidates spent about fourteen billion dollars on their campaigns. Over six and a half billion of that was spent on the presidential campaigns of Joe Biden and Donald Trump.

Kamala's date was with Doug Emhoff. Doug was an entertainment lawyer with two children, Cole and Ella, from a previous marriage. What Kamala liked about him was his honesty, the fact that he didn't feel he had to boast and show off. When he felt he was a bad driver, he told her so. He wasn't arrogant, he was open and comfortable with himself. In a world full of show-off politicians, that must have come as a nice change. A quick phone call turned into an hour, with plenty of laughter. And there were no boring, time-wasting games about who liked who more – Doug sent her a list of his available dates immediately and told her he liked her and wanted to see more of her.

Kamala's first big test, two months later, would be what Doug's children, Cole and Ella, thought of her. Because Kamala's parents had got divorced, she knew how it felt when your parents started dating someone else. So she waited until she thought her relationship with Doug had a chance of lasting, before meeting them.

Kamala took a box of cookies as a present to her first meeting with Cole and Ella, and they all went out for a meal. Afterwards, they invited her to an art show at their school. It was a good sign – and things went well after that too. What Kamala's team thought of Doug was the next big test. How would he manage as a politician's husband, turning up to speeches and events and being supportive? Luckily, Kamala's team loved him – and they loved how he made her laugh.

Whereas Kamala's heritage is Indian and Jamaican, and she attends a Baptist church, Doug is Jewish. When Doug and Kamala married on 22 August 2014 , they had a ceremony that included both Indian and Jewish elements. Kamala put a flower garland around Doug's neck, a Hindu tradition, and he stepped on a glass, which is a Jewish marriage tradition. Their family, with its mixture of cultures, is one which lots of people in today's USA can recognize. Kamala also gets on well with Doug's ex-wife, Kerstin, calling her an "incredible mother". The three team up together to make sure their family works well for Ella and Cole, who are now young adults. Ella said in an interview with *The New York Times*, that "They are really a unit, like a three-person parenting squad. It's really cool."

Cole and Ella decided not to call her "stepmom", but instead "Momala", to rhyme with Kamala. Kamala Harris has described it as "the title I am proudest of". Kamala always makes time to get the family together to prepare Sunday dinner: "As long as I'm making Sunday family dinner, I know that I'm in control of my life – doing something that matters for the people I love."

DIVIDED STATES OF AMERICA

The Favourite: 2016 elections

··

"OPTIMISM IS THE FUEL DRIVING EVERY FIGHT I'VE BEEN IN."

Kamala Harris, interview with
ELLE Magazine (2021)

As 2016 approached, the Democrat senator, Barbara Boxer, who had held the Senate seat for California since 1993, announced she would retire. Politicians across California pricked up their ears. The Senate was the upper house of Congress, a small, important group of elected representatives who made the laws in the USA. Each state had two senators, and they were there for as long as they wanted to be – so there was hardly ever a vacancy in the powerful Senate. But to win in a race like this, you needed plenty of support from powerful people.

After the experience of fighting elections as an elected prosecutor, Kamala felt ready to run for Senator for California. It would give her a seat at the Senate in Washington, DC. It would give her a voice to speak for the people of California at a national level, and the power to influence decisions that affected the entire country. If she won, she would be only the second Black woman ever elected to the United States Senate. She immediately started her campaign, hiring the best people to work for her and raising money. By now, she was an expert in winning elections.

THE UNITED STATES SENATE

The Senate is one of the two parts of Congress, the branch of the American government that makes laws (the legislative branch). The other part is called the House of Representatives.

Capitol building

Senators each represent one of the fifty states of the USA, and each state has two senators, making one hundred in total. They are elected for six years and meet in the Capitol building in Washington, DC to discuss and debate suggested changes to the law. They take a vote on any proposed changes or new laws, and the majority wins. When the Senate is split equally between Republican and Democrat senators, it can be extremely difficult to get any new laws passed, because the two parties often simply block each other's ideas. For this reason, Republican and Democrat senators often have to work together on issues they personally believe in to make things happen. The vice president can cast a vote in the Senate to break a tie.

The way that Californian Senate elections work means that voters often have to choose not between a Republican or a Democrat, but between two people from the same party: a situation that puts people who actually have a lot in common up as rivals against each other. That was the case for Kamala: she ended up facing off against fellow Democrat Loretta Sanchez. Whichever of them won, it would make history. California had never had a Senator who was either a Black or a Latina woman.

By this time, however, a lot of powerful people thought that Kamala was the right woman for the job, and were on her side. She was backed by the California Democratic Party, who gave her over

$700,000 in funding. She was also backed by President Barack Obama, by his vice president, Joe Biden, and by many others including the outgoing senator herself, Barbara Boxer. Kamala looked set to succeed.

But the California Senate elections were only part of the story that was unfolding in 2016. President Barack Obama had come to the end of the two terms that he was allowed to serve, and that meant there was a race for president at the same time. That race was shaping up to be a very bumpy ride.

A Split Country

The most powerful people in the Democratic Party had high hopes that Hillary Clinton, a respected lawyer and wife of previous president Bill Clinton, would become the USA's first female president. She was the obvious choice for Democratic candidate for the president – but as she campaigned, it seemed that a lot of ordinary Democrats disagreed. In the USA, politicians too often came from just a few powerful, wealthy families. Hillary Clinton, voters thought, was another of these politicians – someone who hadn't spent enough time living like an ordinary person to be able to understand them and their problems. Democrat voters preferred a more left-wing politician, Bernie Sanders, who argued for more free health care, creating jobs in tackling climate change, and reducing spending on the military. It was a hint that many voters wanted real change. The question was, what form would that change take? On the Republican side someone who could not have been more different from Bernie Sanders was shouting for the voters' attention – Donald Trump.

Bernie Sanders

Donald Trump was a billionaire who inherited a strong property business from his father, and developed it into luxury hotels, skyscrapers, golf courses and more. He had become a celebrity on TV shows like *The Apprentice*. He had run for president once before in 2000, for the Reform Party, but withdrew from the race because of lack of support. Now, it seemed, his moment had come. He had come into the race for Republican nominee late, and was running against much more experienced politicians. At first most people thought it impossible he could become the Republican Party's choice for president. His style was aggressive and arrogant. He mocked people with disabilities, boasted of assaulting women and grabbed everyone's attention by claiming he would build a physical wall between the USA and Mexico to stop South American people coming to look for work in the USA. He fought with the newspapers and media, calling every report that was critical of him "fake news". Instead, he used social media – Twitter – to communicate directly with people and spread the message he wanted, whether it was true or not.

To Kamala, and to many others in the USA, what Trump was offering the country didn't look like greatness. It looked like bullying on a big scale. The president's actions would set an example to the whole of the USA and show the rest of the world what sort of country they were. Was this really the country they wanted to be?

Perhaps it was, because Trump quickly gained support. His supporters liked it when he told them he would "Make America Great Again". They liked his ideas and thought he could create jobs in their communities again – after all, he was a billionaire, surely he knew how to bring money in? Many of his voters came from poor areas of the USA. They were mostly white and didn't feel that changes over the past years had helped them at all.

The presidential election was a competition between extremes, showing the big divisions and disagreements among Americans about what sort of country they should be.

The Race to Be Forty-fifth

Donald Trump appealed to many voters who no longer trusted politicians. But many others thought that the things he said and tweeted encouraged racism. Whether he was racist or not, racists voted for him. Many voters were bored and mistrusting of experienced politicians and didn't believe that they could provide the change they needed. To many, Trump was interesting, and different. He said things that some voters wanted to hear, and made them feel good about themselves. But would people really vote for him to be president?

To Kamala, Trump stood for the complete opposite of what she believed in. She fought to defend victims of abuse; President Trump boasted of assaulting women. She weighed her words carefully, as a trained lawyer, and made decisions based on evidence and fact; he used Twitter to shout opinions that were often simply untrue. Even many people in his own party thought he was a bad choice. Some formed a movement called Stop Trump to try and stop him getting the presidential nomination. They watched in horror, as did the Democrats, as Trump steamrollered his way to the Republican nomination for president.

Meanwhile, Hillary Clinton had been chosen as the Democrats' candidate for president. Now Donald Trump and Hillary Clinton had to go up against each other to try and gain the support of voters across the USA. It was a vicious campaign, but it looked like Hillary Clinton was just a bit more popular. However, then the FBI, the US secret service, announced that they had investigated Hillary Clinton's handling of secret government material and judged her to have been "extremely careless". No-one wanted a president who would be careless with national security. Even so, the polls projected a win for Hillary Clinton – right up until election day itself. Americans and the world watched as the results came in. Donald Trump had been elected forty-fifth president of the USA.

Hillary Clinton

HOW DOES GOVERNMENT WORK IN THE USA?

There are three parts to government which are supposed to check and balance each other, so that no one part ever gets too much power.

The president is the head of state and the commander in chief of the armed forces. Most of his power is controlled by Congress and the Supreme Court, but he can make some **"executive orders"**. Donald Trump used a lot of executive orders to get things done that Congress did not agree with.

The Supreme Court is the highest court in the land. It can review the decisions of other courts if their decision is questioned. There are nine judges and they have their position for life.

Congress has two parts:

The Senate They discuss and debate the most important matters, such as national security.

The House of Representatives There are 435 representatives who are directly elected by their voters. Each state has a different number, depending on how big their population is. They can vote on how money is used by the government.

Trump's America: 2017–2020

"ANYONE WHO CLAIMS TO BE A LEADER MUST SPEAK

LIKE A LEADER. THAT MEANS SPEAKING WITH INTEGRITY AND TRUTH."

Kamala Harris, Instagram™ post (2019)

The results were in – Kamala had been elected Senator for California, one of the USA's largest and most powerful states. However, as she and her family and friends celebrated at a party for her supporters in a nightclub in Los Angeles, they were also watching the national news report on the presidential elections. Votes were coming in, and the mood quickly turned to concern as Donald Trump edged closer and closer to a win. Finally, it was announced. Instead of choosing Hillary Clinton to be the first female president of the USA, the American people had instead chosen to vote in the Republican, Donald Trump, as forty-fifth president of the USA.

It was one thing to lose to a Republican candidate who was an honourable and responsible leader, but Donald Trump did not give Kamala, or many others, that confidence. Kamala had a speech ready to celebrate victory that evening, but this did not feel like victory. However, she knew that this was not the moment to give up. Her career as a prosecutor had prepared her for losing as well as winning battles she cared about. Her life experience of civil rights activism and protest had taught her that fighting for what you valued was an ongoing struggle. Instead of giving the victory speech she had prepared she got up and told her supporters: "I intend to fight".

Becoming a Senator

As important as the job of being senator was, she knew it had taken on even more importance now that Donald Trump, not Hillary Clinton, was president. Kamala had come from a family that fought for civil rights and defended minorities and vulnerable people, and she had taken that fight into her work as a lawyer and a politician. She could expect President Trump to work for everything she disagreed with – and she would have to push back against it. Her voice was more important than ever.

But first, she had to learn how to be a senator. There were plenty of rules to follow and remember, which the Senate had built up in its more than three hundred years of history. She had to set up her office in just a few days, hiring staff who would be loyal, reliable and great at their jobs. Being a senator for California also meant travelling back and forth frequently from Washington, DC on the east coast of the USA to California on the west coast, an exhausting five-hour flight with three hours of time difference. And Doug had to learn how to be a senator's partner – there was a whole guidebook on it!

Being a senator meant representing your voters at national level, discussing, debating and voting on laws that affected the entire country. Senators helped decide which local governments would get funding and what they would get funding to do and what powers agencies like the FBI would have. The Senate could block or pass laws on women's rights, and vote on who would get elected to the highest court in the country, the

Supreme Court of Justice.

Senators got to join committees, which were groups of people interested in the same area of importance. One of Kamala's most important jobs was joining the Senate Judiciary Committee. This was a group of senators who look after civil rights, voting rights, housing discrimination and other Justice Department enforcement efforts that greatly affect Black Americans. She became only the second Black woman to join that committee, and tweeted that she was: "Thrilled to share that I've been appointed to the Senate Judiciary Committee. You have my commitment that I will fight for justice on behalf of Californians and all Americans."

She could also vote on foreign policy, which was all about how the USA should behave to the rest of the world. As well as the Judiciary Committee, Kamala joined the Intelligence Committee and the Homeland Security Committee, which both looked at ways of defending the USA at home and strengthening it abroad. She learned about new threats like attacks on cyber security – for example, she was shocked to find out that Russia had interfered in the election, encouraging a Trump victory. This news showed Kamala how easy to influence American elections were, and how unprepared they were to deal with cyber threats. That had to be fixed!

Because the Senate was usually split into about half and half Republican and Democrat, senators often had to work with each other to get important laws voted for even though they were not part of the same party. Kamala enjoyed this part of the job, finding common ground with people she usually disagreed with. Across the rest of the USA, that unity and common ground was proving difficult to find.

A Nation Divided by its President

President Trump's election astonished and shocked the world. Newspapers called it a "stunning upset". *The New Yorker* described it as "a tragedy for the American republic." German newspaper *Die Welt* simply asked "How Could This Happen?". In the USA and across the world, the papers said the same thing: this election had showed everyone how divided the USA was. America had gone from voting in the first Black president, to voting in a president who had strong support among racists and white supremacists, and didn't seem to think before he tweeted words that could start a riot. Many, including Kamala, were deeply worried that he was encouraging the divisions in the nation, pushing people further apart from each other instead of helping them see what they had in common.

Those divisions in the nation became a full-blown earthquake in Charlottesville, Virginia in 2017. A rally called Unite the Right took place, with racist, white supremacist groups all coming together in a show of strength. They chanted racist slogans and carried racist, anti-Islamic and antisemitic symbols and flags, including the swastika (the symbol of the Nazi party). They were met by counter-protestors from anti-racist groups, who were determined not to let the rally go without a challenge. The event became violent as the two groups argued and fought.

Then one of the white supremacists drove his car into a crowd of anti-racist protestors. One person was killed and nineteen were injured.

In the hours and days that followed, President Trump was criticized for not clearly condemning the white supremacists. Presidents should unite the country and keep the peace, but also speak up when something is wrong. Donald Trump spoke as if the anti-racists and the racists were just people who disagreed with each other, and he did not make it clear that racism and white supremacy were wrong. To some, he even gave the impression that he agreed with the racists.

Kamala was as horrified as anyone else. The gains in civil rights that Black Americans had made over the years were important, but there were many racists and white supremacists in the USA who would like to see those rights taken away. As a senator, she would have to do everything she could to push back against President Trump's actions. The Senate was mostly filled with Republicans, which meant it was hard for Democrats like Kamala to get the laws through that they wanted to. But she had the power to ask President Trump's officials hard questions about their actions, and she did so, using her experience as a prosecutor to the utmost. She also introduced the bill that led to the Justice in Policing Act of 2020, which was designed to make police officers more accountable for their actions, and also gave the US Department of Justice and attorney generals more power to investigate whole police departments which were suspected of discrimination.

Helping Immigrants

"OUR COUNTRY WAS BUILT BY MANY HANDS, BY PEOPLE FROM EVERY PART OF THE WORLD."

Kamala Harris, *The Truths We Hold* (2019)

In her first speech in Senate, Kamala spoke of her mother, who was an immigrant, and called out President Trump on the things he had done to make the country less welcoming, and life more dangerous, for immigrants. In particular, he had used executive orders to ban any travel into the USA from a few, mainly Muslim, countries, and to order a wall built between the USA and Mexico.

Many children in the USA had been brought there without legal right to stay. They were in school, making friends and living as Americans. Many of them did not remember another home and had come from dangerous places as a baby or very young child. Previous governments had agreed that these children were not to blame for being brought here, and should be given a chance to get legal status and become citizens.

A programme called Deferred Action for Childhood Arrivals (DACA) was in place to help those children live safely in the USA. Donald Trump's government was trying to end DACA. However, he also offered to make a new programme which would let undocumented children become American citizens at some point. But there was a catch – alongside that he also wanted the Senate to let him have $25 billion to build a wall across the USA/Mexico border. Senators could not have one without the other.

Kamala refused to vote for it. She thought the wall was a colossal waste of money, would not secure the border, and also sent the wrong message about what kind of country the USA was. They already had a symbol for immigrants – the welcoming Statue of Liberty! It was frustrating not to be able to do more, but as long as most senators were in the Republican Party, they would support President Trump.

Statue of Liberty

Kamala Harris For The People: 2020 Presidential Campaign

. . . .

"WHAT I WANT YOUNG WOMEN AND GIRLS TO KNOW IS: YOU ARE POWERFUL AND YOUR VOICE MATTERS."

Kamala Harris, interview with
Marie Claire magazine (2019)

Most presidents got to spend two terms in office: Kamala and many other politicians were determined not to let Donald Trump spend more than one term there. As the end of Donald Trump's first term in office approached, Kamala decided to run for president.

In order to become president of the USA, you have to be born an American citizen, be at least thirty-five years old and have lived in the USA for fourteen years. Kamala ticked all those boxes! The next step was to campaign all across the country, to try and get people in her party, the Democrats, to support her as their first choice for president. Like many candidates, she wrote a book to let people know who she was, what her roots and values were, and what she would do if they voted for her. *The Truths We Hold: An American Journey* was her second book, a mixture of memoir and information about what she believed in.

Things had changed a lot since Shirley Chisholm's days, but it was still difficult to be a Black woman running for president. The encouragement Donald Trump had given to white supremacists over his time in office had made Kamala's life more dangerous. Throughout her presidential campaign, Kamala had to travel with full security, receiving threats to her safety that were considered "credible", meaning they really could happen. Kamala crossed the country, joining in debates with the other presidential candidates. Lots of people were impressed by what they saw and heard. As always, her family supported her and worked on the campaign with her.

However, behind the scenes her campaign was running out of funds. It cost a lot to carry

Kamala and her team across the country, to buy advertising and interviews. American politics was a game of money, and if your supporters did not contribute enough money to your campaign you could not get your message out there.

Each political party would meet for a pre-election vote to decide who they wanted to support in a run for the presidency. Having seen all the candidates, the Democratic Party members all met to discuss and debate who was the best and who they really wanted to be their president. Then they cast their votes. That was where Kamala's race for president came to an end in 2020. She was not selected. It was a disappointment, but that was politics – sometimes you won and sometimes you didn't. She thanked everyone who supported her and asked them to vote instead for her favourite candidate who had got through – Joe Biden.

Democratic party logo

Winning a Different Race

"KAMALA KNOWS HOW TO GOVERN. SHE KNOWS HOW TO MAKE THE HARD CALLS. SHE IS READY TO DO THIS JOB ON DAY ONE."

Joe Biden, introducing Kamala Harris as his running mate, *NBC News* (2020)

It was the end of the road for Kamala's bid for president – but it turned out to be the beginning of a new path. Joe Biden was chosen as the Democrats' presidential candidate. The next question was: who would he pick as his "running mate", the person who would become vice president if he became president? It turned out that Kamala's impressive performance in the presidential candidate debates had not been wasted. He offered the position to her.

Kamala recalled what the phone call was like:

"Instead of going on as some might with their involvement with themselves, immediately [Joe] said, 'So, you want to do this?', He just got right to the point. That's who Joe is."

A lot was at stake in this election. By late 2020, the world knew about a new virus, which was highly contagious and was killing people. It was named Covid-19 and as the USA prepared for a presidential election, it was spreading fast across the world. Although relatively few people got very ill from it, millions still did and hospitals were overloaded.

It was a challenge that most politicians had not even thought about, and President Trump was no exception. While other countries raced to stop people mixing and spreading the virus and went into "lockdown", telling people to stay home from work and school, the USA seemed to be doing nothing. President Trump seemed to prefer to pretend the pandemic wasn't happening – but more and more people were falling ill, filling up hospital beds. It was a crisis that, in her first speech as the Democratic nominee for vice president, Kamala recognized: "America is crying out for leadership," she said. "Yet we have a president who cares more about himself than the people who elected him. A president who is making every challenge we face even more difficult to solve". She went on to put it even more starkly: "We need more than a victory on November 3rd. We need a mandate that proves that the past few years do not represent who we are or who we aspire to be."

Now Joe Biden and Kamala Harris were on the same team, competing against President Donald Trump and Vice President Mike Pence. American citizens understood how serious things were and they turned out in their millions to vote for the candidates they preferred. More people voted than in any other election since 1900.

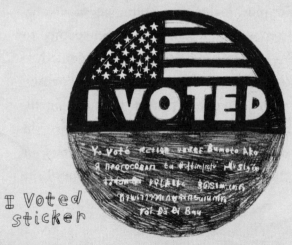

I Voted
sticker

For Joe and Kamala, it paid off. They got 81 million votes – the most votes ever in a US presidential election. Donald Trump became the first president in twenty-eight years not to win a second term. However, Donald Trump and Mike Pence still got more than 74 million votes. There was still a lot of support for him even after the last four years.

So, although the victory was a huge relief for Kamala, when she walked on to the podium in Delaware to accept the congratulations of the Democratic Party at being elected vice president, she did not play down the seriousness of the situation. "America's democracy is not guaranteed," she told them. It was under threat and it needed protection. "We, the people, have the power to build a better future." In her historic speech, she paid special tribute to her mother, Shyamala, who had come to the USA as an immigrant, and to all women who had worked to get voting rights. "While I may be the first woman in this office, I will not be the last," she said, acknowledging the incredible victory of being the USA's first female vice president. With a woman as vice president, there was the hope of one day having a woman as president too.

PRESIDENT JOSEPH ("JOE") ROBINETTE BIDEN JR

Joe Biden was born in Pennsylvania and moved to Delaware when he was a child. Following a career as a lawyer, he was elected as Senator for Delaware. This victory was followed by an awful tragedy when, in 1972, just after he had been elected to the Senate, his wife, Neilia, was involved in a car crash. Neilia and their one-year-old daughter were killed, and their two sons, Beau and Hunter, were badly injured.

Joe was heartbroken and considered resigning his Senate seat after the accident, but was persuaded not to. In 1975, he met his second wife, a teacher called Jill Tracy Jacobs. He went on to be Democrat senator for Delaware until 2009, when Barack Obama selected him as vice presidential candidate. He was the forty-seventh vice president under Barack Obama and was elected forty-sixth president of the USA in 2020.

Joe Biden

Joe believes in combating climate change and wants to invest in green energy, to create jobs at the same time. In joining the 2020 presidential campaign, he said he stood for two things: workers that built the USA and the values that bring the USA together. As president, he has so far focused on getting the USA vaccinated against Covid-19, supporting people who lost their jobs because of the pandemic, reversing many of Donald Trump's executive orders, and dealing with ongoing issues like illegal immigration.

The Attack on Capitol Hill: 2021

"OUR COUNTRY HAS NEVER FULLY ADDRESSED THE SYSTEMIC RACISM THAT HAS PLAGUED OUR COUNTRY SINCE ITS EARLIEST DAYS. IT IS THE DUTY OF EVERY AMERICAN TO FIX."

Kamala Harris, *"To Be Silent Is to Be Complicit"*, article for *Cosmopolitan Magazine* (2020)

In the four years he was in power, President Trump had made it clear he didn't want to be a conventional president. Still his reaction to losing the election was like no other president's had ever been. He refused to accept the result of the election, accusing officials of rigging the vote. There was no evidence for this, and after investigations were carried out, still no evidence. One by one, Republican politicians started to edge away from Trump, embarrassed by his desperation to stay in power no matter what. Still, he refused to admit he had lost, and this gave his supporters belief that he would continue to serve a second term. Some believed in a fantasy story, spread by social media, which said that Trump was fighting against evil people. None of it was real, but it had horrifyingly real consequences that cost lives.

On 6 January 2021, when Kamala and Joe Biden were just two weeks from their inauguration, President Trump called thousands of his supporters to Washington, DC. He made a speech in which he falsely claimed that the election had been "stolen" from him and told his supporters: "If you don't fight like hell, you're not going to have a country any more." Presidents were supposed to unite the country, keep people safe and respect voters' decisions, but Donald Trump was instead whipping up his supporters into believing that they had been cheated.

What followed was shocking, but given the president's encouragement, not surprising. The crowd walked down to the Capitol, where the elected politicians were at work counting the votes that would make Joe Biden president. They quickly overwhelmed the few police who were guarding the building and broke in. Some rioters had come armed with weapons including guns and pipe bombs.

Politicians were hastily taken to safety by the Capitol police, with some quick-thinking officials managing to take the votes they had been counting, so the rioters could not destroy them. They had been right to worry. When rioters got into the building, they smashed and stole property. They chanted "Hang Mike Pence", the Republican vice president, who had refused to continue supporting Donald Trump's claims to have won the election. They looted and vandalized Democrat House Speaker Nancy Pelosi's office. The whole world watched on TV in disbelief and fear, as rioters filmed themselves – and journalists filmed them – invading the building. It looked like the end of the USA's democracy.

Kamala was not at the building. Security forces had warned her in the morning that there might be violence due to the Trump rally, and as the vice president elect, she could be in danger. For some people, to have a Black vice president, who was also a woman and the child of immigrants, was not "their America".

Five people died in the riots – one police officer, and four rioters. Over 138 police officers were hospitalized. One Black police officer, Eugene Goodman, was filmed bravely risking his life in circumstances that could not have been more dangerous to him – a Black man in front of a mob of white supremacist terrorists egged on by their president – drawing the mob towards himself and away from the politicians.

In the end, the rioters were cleared from the building, and the votes were confirmed, making Joe Biden president and Kamala Harris vice president. Republican politicians forced

Trump – their own president – to agree to allow Joe Biden to take power without more protests. Kamala later said in an interview: "We witnessed an assault on America's democracy, a day when we witnessed the terror that a few can wreak on so many … It will be in history recorded as one of the worst days in terms of an attack on the integrity of our democracy."

Above all, the riot had showed Kamala and everyone else who was watching that, if the USA was truly to be a united country and a country without racism, there was still a lot of work to do.

Inauguration Day

On the evening before Inauguration Day 2021, Joe Biden led a ceremony to remember the many people who had lost their lives in the Covid-19 pandemic. It was a sombre start to an event that came with a mixture of emotions.

On the day itself, guests arrived at the Capitol wearing the face masks that were now a common sight. Previous presidents, George W Bush, Bill

Clinton and Barack Obama were there with their wives, Barbara Bush, Hillary Clinton – who had once hoped to be the USA's first woman president – and Michelle Obama. Donald Trump had chosen not to be there, but his vice president, Mike Pence, was.

As happy as they were to be celebrating, invisible threats hung over the day. No-one could escape the thought that the repeated threats of attacks on the inauguration itself would become a reality. The divisions in the USA had not gone away.

Then there was the virus. Usually, hundreds of thousands of tickets were handed out to the public. But this year, none were. Planners of the event had asked people not to come to the capital for fear of spreading the virus. Instead of a long parade, where the virus might spread, there was a one-block military escort for the president and vice president. Virtual events were arranged on TV and social media.

However, there were performances and stars – Lady Gaga sang the national anthem and Jennifer Lopez performed. The surprising star of the day was young poet Amanda Gorman, whose powerful performance of her poem, *The Hill We Climb*, brought her worldwide attention.

Amanda Gorman

And for women all over the USA there was a sense of triumph as the new vice president stepped forward, smiling broadly, to take her oath. Kamala was escorted by the police officer whose bravery had kept rioters away from the politicians during the attack on Capitol Hill. With a hand on a Bible that had once belonged to her hero, Thurgood Marshall, Kamala took her oath: "I do solemnly swear that I will support and defend the Constitution of the United States against all enemies, foreign and domestic; that I will bear true faith and allegiance to the same; that I take this obligation freely, without any mental reservation or purpose of evasion; and that I will well and faithfully discharge the duties of the office on which I am about to enter. So help me God."

It was a triumphal moment in a day whose overwhelming message was: Americans must work to keep democracy and unite their country.

CONCLUSION:

A Future President for the People?

As Kamala took her oath of office, many Americans wondered if they were seeing not just a new vice president, but a future president of their country. Joe Biden is the oldest elected president ever. At seventy-eight years old when he took office, it is no secret that he might not run for a second term after his first four years were up. Perhaps the first female president would also be a Black woman? She was still young for a politician – only fifty-six years old. Everyone watching inauguration day knew that vice president might not be the end of her journey. After all, the vice president often went on to become president themselves, just like Joe Biden had.

By selecting the much younger Kamala, who had made her own bid for the presidency, as his vice president, President Biden seemed to many to be suggesting that the time might soon be right for her to be president of the USA. Despite their age difference and their different life experiences, the two work closely together as a team who seem to respect and like each other. President Biden has said he wants Kamala to be "the last voice in the room" influencing him before he makes big decisions, and to challenge him when she thinks he has got things wrong. With the USA facing many crises in the coming years, from race relations to Covid-19, Kamala may well be a highly influential vice president and have the chance to make her mark on the USA.

Biden's Oval office

Since becoming vice president, however, Kamala has put any of that kind of speculation to one side. She wants to be a loyal supporter of President Biden, in the same way that he supported President Obama, not someone who is seen as trying to take his job. As vice president, she has taken on many responsibilities already, including getting women back into jobs and helping Black-owned businesses that have been badly affected by the pandemic. One of her most important responsibilities has been looking into the migrant crisis, to try and find solutions. Many people come to the USA fleeing violence in South America. They need help, but border guards cannot cope with the number of people trying to get into the USA illegally. Kamala hopes to find a way to help improve the system.

Kamala represents a new kind of American society. She is a Black woman who understands the concerns of Black Americans. She is also the child of immigrants, raised by an Indian mother. Many Indian Americans have seen her as someone who represents them, and have been eager to vote for her. People that haven't showed up to elections in the past have even been more likely to vote because they can choose a candidate who they know has shared their life experiences and culture. They loved the fact that she has constantly paid tribute to her mother, who was born in India. After Mexico, most people in the USA who were born in another country were born in India.

Her career so far has been all about keeping people safe, something all Americans, whatever their identity, care about. She has shown that you can be true to all parts of yourself. That you can be tough and still care about protecting vulnerable people. And that you can lead at the highest level as a woman. She can be an inspiration to all Americans, but especially Black Americans, women and girls, mixed-ethnicity people and immigrants, who can recognize part of themselves in her.

As a woman of colour who achieved many firsts in her time, Kamala has had to get along with a wide range of people. It is hard to please everyone. To some people, she is too much of a change-maker; to others, she doesn't make change fast enough. However, to find common ground with everyone from Democratic activists to Republican senators, without changing your values, and keeping enough people on your side to get as far as vice president, is an extraordinary achievement. All this, while breaking barriers as a "first" woman of colour in a hugely demanding career where every single day brings difficult decisions. Whatever you think of her views and whether or not she becomes president in the future, Kamala is certainly someone exceptional, who has achieved incredible things with a larger-than-usual helping of grit, determination, toughness, and a powerful ability to lead with a big smile. This life story is very far from over.

The White House

KAMALA HARRIS'
CAREER TO DATE:

1986: Graduates from Howard University with a BA in political science and economics

1990: Graduates from law school at the University of California, Hastings, to qualify as an attorney (lawyer)

1990: Joins the Alameda County District Attorney's Office

1998: Becomes managing attorney in the San Francisco District Attorney's Office

2000: Becomes chief of the Division on Children and Families for the San Francisco City Attorney's Office

2003: Elected twenty-seventh District Attorney of San Francisco. In this city in California, residents vote for their top prosecutor, just as they do for their representatives in government.

2010: Elected California's thirty-second attorney general: chief of the largest state justice department in the United States

2017: Elected Senator for California

2020: Runs for the Democratic Party's presidential nomination, but drops out when it becomes clear she does not have enough support. Joe Biden wins the presidential nomination.

2020: Selected by Joe Biden to be his "running mate" in the race for president. Biden and Harris go up against Trump and Pence.

2021: Inaugurated as vice president of the USA

GLOSSARY

Abolish To get rid of something completely

Antisemitic Prejudiced against Jewish people

Anti-Islamic Prejudiced against Muslims

Assault The crime of physically attacking someone

Candidate Someone who puts themselves forward to be voted for in an election

Caste A tradition (especially in Hindu society) which divides people into life-long social classes

Civil Servant Someone who works for the government, but not as a politician. Civil servants carry out policies at a local or federal level.

Concede Agree that you have lost a competition

Democratic A system of government where ordinary people get to vote for their leaders

Desegregate Stop something being separated, often on the basis of race

Discriminate To treat someone worse than others without a good reason, especially treating someone unfairly based on their race, sex or other identity characteristic

Election When a country or organization votes to choose (elect) which party or person will lead them

Endocrinology The science of chemicals in the body called hormones

Freshman Someone in the first year of study, especially at university as an undergraduate

Inauguration A ceremony in which a person who has been elected leader is formally given those powers and takes over. The US presidential inauguration takes place a few months after the election. This is to give the previous president time to move out and the new president a chance to learn how things work.

Integrity Honesty and strong moral principles

Mandate An official order or demand. A mandate from the voters means that a politician has a clear majority of the vote which shows they have strong support to do what they promised.

Memoir A story someone writes about their own life

Migrant Someone who travels from their home to another country

Pandemic An outbreak of a disease that spreads over a whole country or the whole world

Prejudice An unreasonable, unfair dislike of someone, often based on a characteristic like their race, ethnicity, religion or sex

Prosecutor A lawyer who brings a case against someone accused of a crime

Senator An elected representative of a state in the USA

Serial Happening one after another, for example a serial robber commits several robberies one after another

Supremacist A person who believes that a particular group, especially one determined by race, religion, or sex, is better or "superior" and should therefore dominate society, having more rights and power than people who do not belong to that group.

Systemic Part of a system. For example, systemic racism is racism that is embedded through laws, traditions or culture within society or an organization. Segregation and apartheid were examples of systemic racism.

Term (of office) The length of time that a person is allowed to hold an official position for, before people vote for someone diffferent. The term of office for American presidents is four years, and no president is allowed to have more than two terms of office.

ABOUT THE AUTHOR

Leila Rasheed is the author of several books for children and teenagers – her first book, *Chips, Beans and Limousines* was a Red House Read of the Year in 2019, and was shortlisted for the Wigan Explore Book award. In the ten years since Leila was first published she has authored several books and series for children. Her latest book, *Empire's End: A Roman Story* was shortlisted for the Tower Hamlets Book award in 2020.

She also set up and runs a new writer development scheme for Black, Asian and Minority Ethnic writers who want to write books for kids, called Megaphone, which is funded by Arts Council England.

INDEX

LOOK OUT FOR

KATHERINE JOHNSON

There
will
always
be
SCIENCE,
ENGINEERING
and
TECHNOLOGY.

And
there
will
always,
always
be
MATHEMATICS

A LIFE STORY

NASA
Mathematician

STEPHEN HAWKING

Without IMPERFECTION neither YOU nor I would EXIST.

A LiFe STORY

Theoretical Physicist

ROSALIND FRANKLIN

Science and everyday life cannot and should NOT be separated.

DNA Pioneer

SERENA
WILLIAMS

WHATEVER
fear
I have
INSIDE
me,

my DESIRE
to WIN is
always
STRONGER.

Tennis
Player

DAVID ATTENBOROUGH

CHERISH the NATURAL WORLD, because YOU'RE a PART of it

...AND you DEPEND on it.

Natural Historian

CAPTAIN TOM MOORE

The sun will shine on you again

and the clouds will go away.

A LiFE STORY

World War Two veteran and fundraiser